CARRYING to TERM

Carrying to Term

A Guide for Parents After a Devastating Prenatal Diagnosis

By Jane Lebak

Philangelus Press
Boston, MA

Carrying to Term: A Guide for Parents After a Devastating Prenatal Diagnosis Copyright © 2017, Jane Lebak.

All rights reserved. No part of this book may be reproduced or transmitted in any form or by any means, electronic or mechanical, including photocopying, recording, or by any information storage and retrieval system, without permission in writing from the publisher. So there.

Cover art by Charlotte Volnek
Rose designs by Rayha Studios

Scripture quotations are from The Catholic Edition of the Revised Standard Version of the Bible, copyright © 1965, 1966 National Council of the Churches of Christ in the United States of America. Used by permission. All rights reserved.

Print version ISBN: 978-1-942133-24-7
Kindle ASIN: B076L2M8K8
Library of Congress Control Number: 2017915582

Other titles by Jane Lebak:

Honest And For True
Seven Archangels: An Arrow In Flight
The Seven Angels Short Story Bundle
Pickup Notes
Half Missing
Bulletproof Vestments
The Boys Upstairs

Table of Contents

Introduction   3
How to use this book ... Address to parents ... Address to friends and family ... Address to professionals assisting the parents

Emily's Story   16
Emily's story ... The Cost of Joy (poem)

Tips: Your Emotions   28
Feeling overwhelmed ... That weird lull in the middle ... Pre-grieving ... Denial ... Hating the pregnancy ... Hating your body ... Fear ... Depression ... "Acting Pregnant" ... Guilt ... Anger ... Gallows humor

Tips: Bonding With Your Baby   41
Journal ... Poetry ... Music ... Catch phrase ... Heartbeat ... Personality ... Art

Tips: Spiritual Issues   50
Faith versus planning ... What faith is not ... Anger at God ... How could God do this to us? ... Your prayer life ... What comforted me ... Bible verses ... more Bible verses ... Mary lost a Son too ... "God, she's pregnant with a dying baby

Tips: Things Your Baby Needs   68
Decisions ... Clothing ... Car seat ... Stuffed animals ... Plaster molds ... Baby blanket ... Baby sling ... Feeding ... A place to put it all ... The thing I didn't mention

Tips: Dealing with Family and Friends   76
Your parents ... Your siblings ... Your marriage ... Sexuality ... So (poem) ... Your other children ... Your friends ... Your pets

Tips: Dealing with People who Just Don't Understand   95
Who are the Clueless? ... Doctors and other medical professionals ... A word of caution ... Random strangers ... Acquaintances ... Internet trolls ... Strategies that should work most of the time ... Clueless friends ... Clueless family ... Stupid things people say

Tips: Practical Issues   113

Superman ... Driving while permanently distracted ... Confusion ... Cooking for two ... Major decisions and other things not to do ... The physical effects of stress ... Hobbies ... Shopping ... Sudden reminders

Tips: The Birth and Birth Plans   122

Have a birth plan ... C-section ... The birth center ... Organ donation ... Siblings ... Relatives and other visitors ... Religious observances ... Photographs and videos ... NILMDtS ... Things to say, sing, and do ... Hospital staff ... A birth plan template

Emily's Birth Plan   141

Her birth plan ... Blue Moon Baby (poem)

Funeral Planning   147

Cost ... Funeral home ... Funny story ... Emblaming ... Cemeteries ... Take another break ... Cremation versus burial ... Transport ... Songs ... The infamous black dress ... Things to put in the casket ... Mementos at the funeral

But What If ...   164

What if the diagnosis was wrong? ... What if the baby lives for a while?

Coping Afterward and Memorial Ideas   174

The hospital ... Sleep ... Flashbacks ... Milk ... Not being postpartum ... Postpartum depression ... Feeling pregnant ... Return of fertility ... March of Dimes ... Physical exam ... Creativity? What's that? ... When the pizza guy knows your phone number by heart ... The cemetery: to go or not to go ... Tomorrow and tomorrow and tomorrow ... Why you may feel out of place at infant loss groups ... You look like you have it all together ... The peak of loss

Memorial Ideas   191

Obituary ... Birth announcements ... Photographs ... Video ... Scrapbook ... Flowers ... Donations ... Gardens ... Corner shelf ... Memory boxes ... The cemetery ... Tattoos ... Naming opportunities ... Wedding ring memorial ... Lock-of-hair locket ... Flower ornaments ...

Carrying Forward   207
The next baby ... Feeling "untrue" .. "Trying again" ... Coping with a follow-up pregnancy ... Going back to the same hospital ... Smells, sights, and hating maternity clothes

The Friends and Family Section   215
If you're reading this ... A quote about Rule One ... Mementos ... Using the babys' name .. Dates, anniversaries, things that will never happen ... The world's best potato salad ... The spontaneous waterworks machine ... Why not to worry about saying stupid stuff ... A few things not to say

The Section for Professionals   227
Respect for the parents ... Listening to the parents' logic ... Computer mode ... Showing vulnerability ... "Warm blanket care" ... Respecting the baby ... Depression ... Unnecessary roughness ... Yes I'm demanding

Our Aftermath   245
"How many children do you have?" ... Carrying forward ... Helping others ... Reaching more for God

Other Resources   253
Websites ... Books

About the Author   257

DEDICATION

I have no idea how you dedicate a book like this. On these pages you're going to read about so many brave and incredible individuals (friends, relatives, medical professionals) and amazing parents and their sweet babies. I leaned on and learned from so many people that this book couldn't have existed without them all.

Somewhere out there is a mom or a dad who has no idea how to make it through to tomorrow, let alone the rest of the pregnancy or the grieving afterward. This parent may be searching for a road through the darkness. They're not even looking for a highway. Any old path will do, as long as they know it comes out on the other side of the woods.

If that's you, this book is dedicated to you and your resolution to do the best you can by your little one.

INTRODUCTION

I am sorry you need this book. I am sorry anyone would need this book.

This book didn't exist when I needed it, so I wrote it. It started as a long mental list I compiled after my baby was diagnosed with anencephaly, then added to it during the months of her pregnancy and during the intensity of the days surrounding her birth and death. A couple of months later, when I wanted to write Emily's story, I didn't want it to be just her story. Her life should help others, but how?

By being someone to lean on. By being a light.

I'll back up a bit. Parents think of prenatal testing as a way to meet their baby ahead of time. Doctors, on the other hand, are looking for problems, and not all of them can be solved. Or rather, the only solution the doctors can offer is to terminate the pregnancy and have the mother try again, as if human beings are interchangeable.

In 2005, for example, there were 6,925 fetal and infant deaths attributed to lethal anomalies in the United States. These include congenital malformations and chromosomal abnormalities. They're called "incompatible with life," and given names as trisomy 13, Potter's sequence, trisomy 18, acrania, and anencephaly (what my daughter had) along with many others. The babies will grow and develop fine while supported by their mother's body, but at birth, they cannot survive on their own, and they often die in minutes or hours.

The majority of these babies are aborted after diagnosis even when the fetal abnormality does not in any way compromise the mother's health. Geneticists and maternal-fetal medicine specialists will often have a dozen books and pamphlets addressing various methods of pregnancy termination, but when the parents continue the pregnancy, they offer nothing more than a statement that they'll continue to offer prenatal care, and then at birth, the parents can watch their baby die.

The situation doesn't have to be this helpless. We can forge a best-case scenario out of a worst-case scenario.

Why? Because that's what parents do. Because short time is not valueless time. Because tomorrow is never a promise, so we need to focus now on how to love a baby we have right now.

Parents can maximize the time they have with their baby. It is possible to bond with a baby who hasn't yet been born. Parents have learned to make memories in very short windows of time. It's possible to organize what's most important and grieve ahead of time so that when you're holding your baby, you're overwhelmed with love rather than shock.

In the confusing time after Emily's death, I cobbled together a website of practical tips for parents who were in the same situation. I wrote it in a fog of determination: my daughter's life had ended, but her impact on the world would not. During the twenty-two weeks between her diagnosis and her birth, my best supports had come from parents ahead of me in the journey. I wanted to help others too, but I'd learned my experience alone wasn't special enough to serve as a light.

Instead I focused on the tactics and strategies my family employed to endure the unendurable. How is it possible to keep loving God when it feels as if God has deceived you? How can you reach out to your community for help? How can you take care of your other children when you can barely take care of yourself? How can your marriage survive a blow that crushes both partners at the same time?

Emily's website got hundreds of hits every month, and shortly I started receiving letters from parents who'd found it helpful. Some after reading my site had even decided not to abort.

I became moderator of a pro-life anencephaly support group on Yahoo for several years, listening to hundreds of women as they endured the same struggles, the same questions. And although our situations were all different, so many of the concerns sounded the same. Concerns about how the older siblings would handle grief. Concerns about husbands and wives with different grieving styles. Concerns about friends who wanted nothing more than to pretend our dying babies never existed.

And mixed with the grief, fear. Fear of whether we'd be able to love our babies despite their physical deformities.

Fear that we wouldn't be good enough mothers when motherhood to this baby was going to be so short.

This book won't pull punches because you've already been sucker-punched about as hard as life can hit. I'm going to treat this book as though it's a support group you can keep in your pocket, and therefore I'm going to share the times I was vulnerable, the times I was laughably wrong, and the times I was pig-headed. (Sometimes being pig-headed can work to your advantage. You should decide on the appropriate level of pig-headedness for any given situation.) In a real-life support group, you usually find that whenever you disclose the worry or the pain that you thought no one else ever experienced, suddenly three heads lift up and someone gasps, "I thought I was the only one."

So here you go. I'll be vulnerable in this book so you know you're not the only one. I'm going to share any number of my failures and flaws because I want you to see that perfection is not required, and neither is it expected.

What I think is required for you to survive this journey is emotional honesty, so be honest with yourself the same way I'm going to be honest with you. When you hurt, admit you're hurting. Feel your pain. Feel your own strange mixture of happiness the baby is here now, while at the same time the grief that the baby won't be here for long. Call every feeling what it is. Honesty is the way toward personal growth, but more importantly, I think it's the only real path to survival right now. Think about a guy carrying a fifty-pound backpack up a mountain. He can either admit it's heavy and try to adjust for the burden, or he can keep telling himself, "No, it's light. It's fine. I can do this," until the moment he crashes to the ground and then—guess what?—has to admit it really was that heavy.

Carrying to Term is based primarily on my experiences: first with my daughter Emily and later moderating the online support group, attending a real-life support group, and reading a billion books (slight exaggeration). The book consists of practical tips for parents who are doing the unthinkable, everything from funeral planning to spiritual struggles to negotiating with hospital regulations to how to pick out a dress for a postpartum funeral when you're still seven months pregnant.

HOW TO USE THIS BOOK

You know how some books have an opening chapter along the lines of "How to use this book"? Well, here's my *How to use this book*: don't feel like you have to use it at all.

I spent the time of my pregnancy planning as much as I could, and planning helped me. I'm passing the planning along in case it helps you.

If a suggestion doesn't help you? Ignore it. I'm not an expert. I'm a mom who has "been there, done that" and who's picked up advice from other moms who've "been there, done that." But I'm not the mom of *your* baby. I'm not living *your* life.

There are as many ways to love and care for a baby in this situation as there are parents in this situation. So if I had any advice on "How to use this book," it would be this:

read and think about the issues I raise, and maybe you'll agree with me and maybe not.

There are no right ways and wrong ways to love your baby.

I always encourage my editing clients to disagree with me because oftentimes that's how they come up with the very best solutions for themselves and the book they're writing. I cite an issue in the manuscript and suggest a fix, and they say, "I have a better way to handle that." Therefore I'm saying the same here: don't do something that's a bad fit for your life or your soul just because you read it in a book. Yes, even this book.

But even when you disagree, I'm still talking about issues you ought to think about. (And yes, when you get to the section on Clueless Advice, you'll chuckle at me saying about my own book, "That certainly is something to think about.")

ADDRESS TO PARENTS

Before I open the fire hose of the tip section, I'm going to share advice from Monika Jaquier, owner of anencephaly.info

When a new anencephalic baby is born, I always think about how it was when I had my little Anouk. What went fine, what could have been better. I hope that the mother who has her baby now does not make the same "mistakes" I did, that she does not have regrets as I have sometimes.

While I was thinking about this, God reminded me of the story of Jesus visiting Martha and Mary (Luke 10.38-42). Martha was cleaning the house, preparing a good meal... all the things which have to be done. Mary sat down at the feet of the Lord and listened to his teaching. Martha was upset and asked Jesus to send Mary to help her. But Jesus said : "You are worried and troubled over so many things, but just one is needed. Mary has chosen the right thing, and it will not be taken away from her."

We are worried over so many things; so many things could have been done better during the time we had our babies.

But God said to me, "Just one was needed." To give all my love to my baby. I didn't give a bath to

> *Anouk, I didn't even try to nurse her... but God comforts me and says, "Just one was needed, and you have done it."*
>
> *The love I gave to Anouk will never been taken away from her!*

Your number one job is to love your baby. You're already doing that.

But keep repeating this to yourself: Rule One is to love your baby. When it feels like you can't go on, even if you have to jettison everything else, fall back to Rule One.

Right now it hurts. Every breath, every day, every reminder hurts. No one knows how to help, and that's because in large part they can't. Your number two job is to get through this, and that's where I'd like to offer my experiences and raise issues.

Don't worry about remembering them all or forming a long-term plan (unless you're a chart-lover and a list-lover, in which case, whoa, make lists and charts!). Instead read through and just immerse yourself. Get an idea in your head of how you'll manage most of the bumps in the road, and then just go ahead and drive.

Have you ever asked a relative for a recipe only to get a blank look? My brother-in-law asked how I make meatballs, and I said, "Oh, you fry up some onion and some garlic, mix it up with some ground beef and ground pork, add breadcrumbs and egg, and then you can either fry them or bake them." When he subsequently pointed out that recipes usually have (you know) measurements, I was forced to agree that this was indeed the case. But it's not how I do things, and I suggest that's not how you do things either.

Control? We can't control the most important things. But we can get a general sense of how we'll handle them and form a general philosophy approaching this time with our babies.

I want you to read through so you won't be surprised when situations come up. I want you to read through so that if you find yourself in a position where you have to advocate for your baby, you've already gotten a sense of how you want to handle it.

If I make you laugh a bit along the way, I'll be glad of that too. Humor was one of my most used coping mechanisms.

In general, though, you're living a worst-case scenario. A little planning might help you to have a best-case-worst-case scenario.

ADDRESS TO FRIENDS AND FAMILY OF THE PARENTS

If you are a family member or a friend of the soon-to-be-bereaved parent, thank you for reading here and learning as much about their situation as possible.

I've included a section for friends and family with tips specific to them, but nothing in this book is "off limits" to anyone, so feel free to read the whole thing if you want.

Don't worry too much about saying and doing the wrong thing. If you're concerned enough to read a whole book about what your loved one is going through, you're probably not going to say anything heartless. Clumsy? Sure. We all do that. Let me reassure you about something: we can tell the difference.

Right after the diagnosis, I called my closest friend and tried to tell her what had happened. I wasn't coherent. She was surprised and stunned too because she didn't even know this kind of situation could happen, and she stumbled through trying to find something to say to me that might help, somehow. At some point in the conversation she said, "At least there are some nice cemeteries up by you."

I'm sure she beat herself up for that afterward. *Nice going,* she must have thought. *She tells you her baby is going to die, and you tell her that at least there will be pretty trees over the grave. Brilliant.*

You know what? What she said saved me from making a horrible mistake choosing the cemetery. Because I was just going to go with the local churchyard, which had the baby graves relegated to the back near a drainage ditch. All the stones were askew, and everything was a mess. I was so upset thinking about leaving Emily there, in that ugly place, and then I remembered my friend. *There are some nice cemeteries up by you.*

So I gave myself a good shake. I found another cemetery. And that's where Emily is now, in a lovely place toward the center of town. There are trees and gorgeous fences, and you can put little statues on the gravestones. In the fall there's a tremendous maple tree that turns redder than any other tree I've ever seen. On some mornings, after I dropped off my older child at preschool, I'd sit there and just listen to the wind and look around at the other graves, and I'd feel at peace.

Moral of the story? Don't worry about saying something dumb. Be present and give them all the love you can right now. They need it.

Thank you for reading here, and I wish you strength as you accompany your loved one on this journey.

ADDRESS TO PROFESSIONALS ASSISTING THE PARENTS

To the doctors, nurses, counselors, ultrasound techs, and everyone else who might read this book: you're in a crucial position right now to a family that really needs you. Maybe this is the first time you've faced an unsolvable problem. Maybe you've never been comfortable with grief. What matters now is that you're here and this family is relying on you.

This book will present examples of both good and bad medical professionals, and by "bad" I don't mean professionals who wrote the wrong dosage on a prescription pad. The bad doctors and bad nurses and bad therapists were the ones who attempted to coerce their patients, whether through mockery or skewed statistics or outright lies. So while I had midwives who walked into the room and gave me a hug (every one of the midwives in that practice hugged me at least once), the professionals that come to mind first are the ones like the doctor who started my friend's appointment by calling her an idiot.

You're reading this book because you're already one of the good ones and want to be one of the best. A doctor or a therapist like you is a treasure. This isn't hyperbole. The ultrasound tech who had us come back on her lunch hour so she could get a few pictures of Emily for us was a *treasure*. The pediatrician who exclaimed, "They damn well better let you hold your baby!" and gave me her phone number to call even if I delivered in the middle of the night? A treasure. Nothing less.

To someone who's just been slapped in the face by the reality that life isn't fair, your extra minutes of time and your compassion will feel like cool relief, and they will trust you. Your emotions will reassure them. Your honesty will be their strength.

Thank you for being here, and thank you for being there for them too.

EMILY'S STORY

When I became pregnant with my second child in October 1999, I prayed that everything would go differently this time. I should have been more specific about what I asked for, because the first time, I left the hospital with a living child.

We wanted this pregnancy. I did all the "right" things. Because we use Natural Family Planning, we knew pretty much when we conceived. In fact, I went to the doctor to get tested too soon! I was sure because I was already having symptoms—the most welcome one the nonstop dreams I'd had every night of the nine months of my first pregnancy. The practice that had delivered my first baby had closed, thankfully, but the doctor who had done the delivery had moved to the only practice in the area that my insurance company paid. I didn't want to get him again.

That was when I started saying I wanted everything to go differently. I read different books, and I changed my attitudes about prenatal care and testing. Because of the high false-positive rate, we didn't have an alpha-fetoprotein test, although we scheduled an ultrasound. After all, an AFP test doesn't tell you about things that are correctable, but an ultrasound theoretically can.

That new practice was... Well, we changed insurance companies so I could leave them. I transferred my records to the new practice only four days before the scheduled ultrasound with the old one, but I no longer cared. The timing was an act of God.

At the time, I didn't realize my body was telling me something was the matter. My nonstop dreams had halted abruptly in mid-November. Before the exam where the doctor was going to hear the heartbeat for the first time, I was so terrified that I didn't bring my son to the appointment. I wasn't telling acquaintances—a real difference from my first pregnancy when I told anyone who didn't get out of my way quickly enough.

Plus, week after week, I wasn't gaining weight. Even after the first trimester and its morning sickness passed, the weight wouldn't come on.

At the beginning of the pregnancy, stepping out of the shower one morning, I remembered an article called "Stephen's Prayer" from the Couple to Couple League's Family Foundations newsletter (back before it was a magazine). In it, a couple had a baby diagnosed with a fatal abnormality, whom they carried to term. Their baby had the same first and middle name as my own first son. As I reached for a towel and remembered the article, a question popped into my head: What would I do if the baby had anencephaly?

Without hesitation, I responded, "I'd have to carry it to term anyhow."

I think that was the Holy Spirit, preparing me.

I had a good ultrasound technician. She must have seen it outright, but she kept up light chit-chat until time came to take measurements. Then she told us to stay in the room for a moment because last week the computers hadn't processed the images correctly; she'd just check and return in a minute. I talked to my husband about how well that had gone. And then the technician returned with the radiologist.

I went cold. I asked if something was the matter. He said to just lie back and he'd retake the measurements.

Then he asked, had I had an AFP test?

I knew there were only a few things an AFP test looked for: twinning, Down's syndrome, spina bifida, and anencephaly. We knew there weren't twins.

He went right for the head.

When I couldn't take the tension any longer, I said to the radiologist, "What is it?"

He said, "Anencephaly."

I whispered, "No brain?"

My husband gasped and turned around. I was numb. I asked how sure he was. He said 100% sure. When was the last time a medical person said "100%" about anything?

I knew a few things about anencephaly. I knew it was incurable. I knew there was no danger to me. I knew it meant our baby would die. In retrospect, I don't know how I knew these things, where I'd read them and why I'd remembered. Maybe again the Holy Spirit.

The radiologist said he'd leave us alone while he called my midwife. I said, "Tell her we're not going to terminate."

The radiologist said, "I'm only going to—"

I was like a madwoman. "Tell her we're not going to terminate!"

And then we were alone. James and I talked quietly and held one another. I couldn't believe it—and yet I could. I don't know what I was feeling, if I even felt anything. I was scared and desperate—but not in denial. For some reason, I never doubted it was all happening.

We got to see the doctor. Because we'd suddenly become a "high-risk" case, we were seeing one of the practice OBs. She wasn't very nice.

She was, in fact, mad that we'd taken the choice out of her hands about whether to terminate. She tried to scare us. She said, "These babies are pretty hideous." She also said, "If we don't induce, you could carry her for fifty-five weeks."

She told me it was outrageous that I'd want to see and hold my baby, and then she said that if I breastfed the baby, even once, my periods might not return for two years. Fortunately (I guess) my experience with the previous OB had taught me something important: some doctors will lie. So I said we were going to get a second consultation with another practice. And I never saw that nasty doctor again.

The radiology tech hadn't taken any pictures from the scan. She hadn't found out the gender. It left me feeling that much more desolate: not only was I not going to have a baby, but now I didn't even have something to hold onto or a way to know about this baby I was going to lose. I was already thinking, "I want my baby back."

In the middle of that night, I woke up and thought about the baby's name. If it was a girl, I didn't want to give her the name we'd planned. In retrospect I shouldn't have done it, but I went for a second-string name my husband had liked during our first pregnancy. Emily. And what about a middle name? It came to me, Rose. No boys' names presented themselves. When my husband woke up, I said, "Emily Rose. If it's a girl." He said, "All right."

My husband called the clinic and asked for copies of Emily's ultrasound pictures. The radiologist said we could come back and take more for free. It took five minutes of the woman's lunch hour, but I hope God blesses her abundantly for that simple kindness. She showed us the anencephaly in more detail, how the top of Emily's head had failed to form above the eyebrows. She took three pictures. And she determined that our baby was a girl.

We got a second opinion. The second radiologist spent 45 minutes confirming the obvious. We spoke to a genetic counselor, and we saw a specialist in high-risk cases. Everyone we met at Dartmouth Medical Center was superb. They never tried to scare us or to push us to terminate. So much for the supposed fifty-five week pregnancy. Back at home, I returned my care to the midwives.

We got the diagnosis at twenty-two weeks. We had five months to prepare our toddler son for what was happening, introduce him to the concept of death, and encourage as much sibling bonding as was possible. I took care of ten million details, just about all of which are preserved somewhere in this book. I joined support groups. I learned every single thing I could.

We prayed. We asked others to pray, and they asked still others. Her name was said at Mass every day at two parishes, and the second-graders at a Catholic school turned every walk into a silent prayer walk for her. We estimate Emily had seven hundred fifty people praying for her!

And I know God answered our prayers. So many things that could have gone wrong, didn't go wrong. The very fact that I'd switched practices before getting the news showed me that God was guiding us. Coincidences, good feelings, and loving support from everyone around us demonstrated that God was walking through this at our sides. What I wanted most of all, I might not get, but at least we weren't struggling all alone.

That meant Emily's anencephaly had a purpose. Hers wouldn't be a wasted life.

I had only one chance to love Emily while she was still in the world. Only twenty more weeks until her due date. We tried to take advantage of all of them.

Emily had her own personality. I didn't understand before those months how a mother can bond before birth—but I tried. How much was imagination and how much fact, I can't tell. But she seemed stubborn. Although the medical professionals asserted she would be both blind and deaf, Emily reacted to sound. More than that, she could react in specific ways to specific words. She disliked noise, and she jabbed furiously when I turned over at night. She kept my husband awake by kicking him when we cuddled, and yet she held totally still whenever her brother touched my tummy.

She put us in mind of Mary in The Secret Garden, solemnly telling Colin, "If everyone thought I was going to die, I wouldn't do it." And we hoped not. We sincerely hoped not.

At 27 weeks, I had what I thought was preterm labor. I managed to get it stopped, but that incident renewed my frenzy to ready everything for my daughter's arrival. By 38 weeks, the details were all taken care of. I was at term. Emily wasn't ready to come out, though. The due date passed. Finally, we set an induction date for 42 and a half weeks.

I can't describe how comforting the midwives were. I received top-notch care and generous understanding. Never was I criticized for carrying my baby to term. They were more than happy to give a little extra hand-holding when I fretted about the fundal height or too-frequent Braxton-Hicks contractions.

We arranged for all three sets of Emily's grandparents to come for her birth. We began the induction at 10 in the morning on July 19th, and Emily was born at 11:08 p.m.

The birth itself was everything I had wanted it to be—everything my first birth was not. I was unmedicated and in control. I felt Emily kicking all the way. Right before I pushed her out, I could feel her turn in the birth canal, and I exclaimed to everyone that she was still moving.

She emerged into the world purplish-grey, still, silent, and not breathing.

The nurses slipped a cap on her head and laid her unmoving body in my arms. My husband quickly grabbed the jar of Lourdes water and pronounced the words of a conditional baptism. "If you are able to be baptized, I baptize you in the name of the Father, and of the Son, and of the Holy Spirit."

Abruptly she gasped, and I exclaimed, "You're alive!" The nurses sprang into action, suctioning her and rubbing her down.

My baby was alive. My baby was here.

I saw with disappointment that all our prayers hadn't healed her, but it didn't matter at that moment. She was here. I was holding her. She was Emily Rose, my daughter. It was all I wanted.

My husband called the family, and everyone had a chance to hold her, including our son. My brother took video while Emily went around the room and met everyone. The Catholic chaplain came and confirmed her.

Everyone took pictures, rolls of pictures. I'd seen photos of other families holding their babies and wondered, "How can these people be smiling?" But in our photos you can see it too, me holding my daughter and smiling. I had Emily, for however briefly. Why wouldn't I smile?

Emily remained with us for two precious hours. During that time, she had an attitude of paying careful attention. She opened only one eye, but she reacted to my voice and the things I said. She was bleeding from her head, though, and in the end she couldn't hang on.

I whispered to her that if she had to go, it was all right—she could go. A little after one in the morning, just as the video tape ran out, she left us.

It wasn't until after Emily was dead that I really inspected her. She had all the right numbers of fingers and toes. She had huge feet, just like her brother, and perfect piano-player hands with long fingers and pretty fingernails.

Her eyes were brilliant cobalt blue, and her hair was dark brown. She weighed six pounds, fifteen ounces, and was nineteen and a half inches long. Her mouth was covered with nursing blisters, I suppose from sucking her fingers in utero, but I couldn't find a matching callous on her hands. Her ears were pressed hard to the sides of her head, also like her brother's had been. Her eyes bugged out a bit because the orbital bones had failed to form properly.

I finally had the courage to remove her cap and look at the damage to her head. Her face stopped right above the eyes: she had no eyebrows at all. There was an open part at the top of her head, about as big as the circle of my thumb and forefinger. Her brain was exposed, covered only by a thin membrane.

Her brain had hemispheres, so the doctors had been wrong when they said only her brain stem would form. She'd had a sucking reflex. She'd had hearing. She might have understood who we were. Our familiar voices might have been a comfort to her.

I looked desperately to find a birthmark on her, wanting something else to remember her by—some feature that was distinctly Emily—but there was none.

The rest of the details are important to me and not so important to anyone else: the night she spent in the bassinet in the hospital room; the way my husband and I held her for one extra hour in the morning before letting the nurse take her away; the way the funeral director brought her to us cradling her in his arms.

What I remember clearest is how many people showed their support and how many strangers made an effort to reach out to us. It's never easy to bury a child, but I think everyone's presence made it less than impossible.

I didn't understand why Emily had to die, but over time I've reached some conclusions. They may not help anyone else; they may, in fact, be totally wrong. But I decided that in some way, Emily's soul needed whatever particular type of love my husband and I were going to give her. And that my soul needed to love Emily. For whatever reason, God saw we needed one another, and therefore God put us together.

I had the privilege of being a mother to a child who would never "benefit" me. God gave me the gift of giving someone unconditional love. How often in our lives do we have such a chance? But in nurturing a baby who wouldn't remain with us, my husband and I had the chance to be like God and love without any anticipation of a return.

I met some very charitable and generous people because of Emily. I hope this book will able to help others the way I was helped during my time of crisis.

THE COST OF JOY

by Jane Lebak

You were made for joy.
Every mother hopes high,
Dreams deep and brave
And waits for the pain.
An ocean dispersed,
A cord cut,
And the new life is pushed upon the shore
Of the outside world.
Nature demands no less.
But nature bites deep
As one by one dependencies fail
And the child ventures afield.
Every step brings its own dangers,
And dangers bring sorrow.
All part of growing.
It starts with a cut cord.
It ends with a cut heart.
Every mother thinks she would stop it
If she could.

There will be no sorrow for you,
Emily Rose.
No danger, no steps away from the source.
I am your shore and your home.

Carrying to Term

The cord cut, the danger comes
All at once.
You were made for joy.
You can't stay.
This world teems with sorrow
And soon so will I.
But you were made for joy.

TIPS: YOUR EMOTIONS

You're in the middle of one of the most emotionally intense periods of your life. "Roller coaster" doesn't even begin to describe it, but I'm going to give it a shot.

FEELING OVERWHELMED

It felt like it was going to be forever until Emily's birth. At least at first.

My experience was that the first two weeks dragged. Without focus, it felt as if every day stretched a thousand miles long, and I couldn't possibly do this thing. Four months? I had to wait four months?

I'd get up, get my son dressed and breakfasted, and then it would overwhelm me: I had a whole day ahead! I could never do that!

But I could make it to snack-time because snack was only two hours away.

After snack, I'd again find myself rudderless, but lunch was again a couple of hours away. I couldn't make it through a whole day, but I could make it to lunch.

With lunch over, I was done. Cooked. Stick a fork in me. But, well, there was another snack coming up in a couple of hours, so...

Anyhow, you get the point. I would hand-over-hand myself to the end of the day, and after dinner I'd think, "Well, another couple hours and I can go to bed," and then the next day I'd do the whole slog all over again.

THAT WEIRD LULL IN THE MIDDLE

Then I got into the swing of things, and the next few months sped far too quickly. Entire weeks would zip by.

Don't get me wrong: even after that point, some days were two hundred hours long. But after a while I had the sense of inevitability: time was passing much too quickly, and I couldn't stop it. Emily was here now, but "now" was getting less and less.

It's kind of odd, but after the diagnosis, the pregnancy consists of months that pass altogether too quickly and too slowly at the same time.

So if you're still reeling from the diagnosis and thinking you can't make it through, hang in there. It'll get easier before it gets harder again.

PRE-GRIEVING

There are web sites and books that give a very good in-depth discussion of grieving, the stages of grief, and a rough-and-ready timetable. You can probably recite the stages yourself ("Denial, Anger, Bargaining, Depression, Acceptance.")

I found they didn't apply very well to me. In fact, most of the moms in our group found the same.

The truth is, we are our own special category. We start grieving from the moment we get the diagnosis. I call it pre-grieving.

Initially there will be shock and numbness. But because we haven't suffered the loss yet, something else happens. We get a chance to answer all the questions that plague the bereaved ("Why?" "Is this my fault?" "How could God do such a thing?") long before we are actually "bereaved."

We're in pain, but we're not struggling with the shock and hysteria that would accompany a more sudden loss. When it gets too much, we have a consolation: the baby is still here. We haven't lost her yet. There's still time.

DENIAL

When I asked the radiologist how sure he was of the diagnosis, he said, "One hundred percent."

Even if part of grief is denial, a lot of us don't get that luxury. Holding an ultrasound photo of your baby, you can see whatever part is missing and can't say, "Well, maybe they're wrong." So speaking only for myself, I found it almost kinder that there was no hope for Emily. I would have hung onto the hope until her last breath—in fact, I did that anyhow. But I wouldn't have prepared for her death until it happened.

It's perfectly acceptable to prepare for your child's death in advance. In the section on funerals, I'll discuss why it's almost essential. For now, suffice it to say that preparing for the worst won't cause the worst to happen.

A lot of parenting is about preparation. You've been denied a lot of the parenting experiences you deserve to have, but you still have the chance to prepare if you choose to do so.

HATING THE PREGNANCY

For a few days, I hated my pregnant body.

I cringed every time Emily kicked. I didn't want to show. I desperately wanted to go into preterm labor just so it would be all over with. For a while, I even stopped wearing maternity clothes.

I've since discovered that this is a common reaction, and that most women I've asked say they felt the same at first. We all want a way out of the pain, a way that's morally acceptable but also quick and easy. Nobody wants to drag out suffering.

For me, once I settled down to the reality that there was no way out, I let go of my search for the "easy way" and felt that any time remaining with Emily was a gift. Then I began to bond with her however I could in whatever time we were granted, and I stopped hating the pregnancy.

In fact, when it seemed as if I really was going into preterm labor, I took measures to stop it, and I was tremendously relieved when they worked. When we finally set the date for Emily's induction at 42.5 weeks, I felt incredibly sad that her time inside, where she was safe, would be ending so soon. Other women tell me they felt the same. So trust me, this will pass.

HATING YOUR BODY

I hated my body too. My body failed Emily. Whatever happened to her, it happened on my watch. She was fine as a zygote and a blastocyst and an embryo. Then one day her neural tube didn't close, and it happened inside me.

I hated my defective body. In a way, I hated me.

If you feel this way, do try to be gentle on yourself.

Imagine a perfectly hateful woman. Imagine she's just totally evil. Now imagine she's pregnant and wants – actually wants – to cause whatever condition your baby has. Guess what? She can't do it. And if she can't do it, you didn't have anything to do with it either. You couldn't have.

Be compassionate with yourself the same way you'd be compassionate with a friend in the same situation. You didn't do this. You didn't cause it. You don't deserve your own hatred.

FEAR

I haven't heard this reaction discussed, although C.S. Lewis begins *A Grief Observed* by saying how surprised he was that grief felt like fear. In my case, I began feeling afraid of everything. Right in the doctor's office after getting Emily's diagnosis, I was afraid that something would happen to my three-year-old son.

Afterward, dozens of old fears resurfaced, and the fear peaked in the month after Emily's death. Scenarios I hadn't feared since childhood returned to my mind. I'd be driving and feel a terror that the car's doors would blow open. Or I'd be afraid the house would suddenly burn down. Or that the fan blade would spin off the fan and hurtle through the room.

I think it was Scott Peck in *The Road Less Traveled* who said the difference between a neurosis and a psychosis is that a neurosis makes you miserable while a psychosis makes everyone else miserable. Well, I tried to keep my fears neurotic, not forcing others to do or not do things based on what I was afraid would happen. I always forced myself to take a deep breath and analyze how likely this particular fear was. Quite often, it was only a result of the stress. And the car doors never did blow open.

DEPRESSION

No one can stop you from feeling sad. Nor, in my opinion, should anyone try. You're about to suffer a loss that will cut into your heart and change who you are for the rest of your life. If you didn't feel sad, people would wonder.

But depression is more than being sad, and as someone who's faced depression too, I know it's not always in our control.

Some parents have found help in antidepressants because that took enough of the edge off the depression that they could process their grief. Others felt it wouldn't help because it would merely numb them to the grieving they needed to be doing.

This is a personal choice, and you need to discuss it with your doctor or midwife if depression is an issue.

With or without medication, there are five things you absolutely must do to stave off mild depression. We'll call it the Lebak Depression Prevention Program because it sounds so...official.

Odds are that you're doing these things anyhow if you're pregnant, and even more if you have other children or employment outside the home. But here's the program:

- Get a shower every day.
- Get dressed every day.
- Get out of the house every day, even if it's only to walk around the block.
- Eat regular meals every day.
- Avoid sugar and alcohol.

Yes, that's very simple. No one's going to write a blockbuster bestseller based on my little list. (Um, I mean, program.) But I found that whenever I've been depressed, it's helped if I made a point of doing all five of these things every day as a means of feeling better.

For some reason, calling it a program makes it more justifiable. Depressed people, especially depressed women, don't always feel they're "worth" a balanced meal (for example). So don't eat because you feel hungry. Eat because it's part of your regimen and someone told you it would help.

If there are any other tactics you find eliminate depression, add them to the program. I found that for me, flossing regularly will lessen a bout with the blues. Why? I have no idea. It's probably all in my head (and not just because my teeth are in my head) but since the only side effect is healthier teeth and gums, I go with it.

But, *and this is very important,* if you ever start feeling self-destructive or incapable of ordinary daily functioning, don't just get a well-balanced meal. Call your doctor. Ask a friend or your spouse for help if you can't make the call yourself, but please do. You're worth taking care of.

"ACTING PREGNANT"

Giving up alcohol, junk food, medication, coffee, cigarettes...it's assumed that every pregnant woman will live a life of virtue and natural healthfulness for nine months. Ice-cream jokes aside, you're "supposed" to eat better while pregnant than you will for the rest of your life.

Even before we got Emily's diagnosis, I'd sometimes pick up the candy and say seriously, "Honey, is this the best possible M&M I could give my baby?" But afterward, it seemed so unfair that I had to give up some of the only comforting things in my life for a baby who wouldn't reap the benefits. What hurt worst was giving up coffee. Why couldn't I just have a beer or a coffee and say it wouldn't matter, that it certainly couldn't hurt Emily's brain development at this point?

Well, you can. No one's going to look askance at you if you relax on the pregnancy protocols.

Personally, I did not. I figured it would have hurt *me*, because in my mind, that would have been giving up. That's what I told myself over and over. I was carrying Emily to term because I wanted her to have the fullest and best possible life she could have. I had to give her whatever I'd give my other children, just out of fairness.

To me, fairness meant continuing to eat healthy, not taking any medications, taking the prenatal vitamins, and all that jazz.

To you, the answer may be different. This is fine.

This is not a moral issue. Relaxing on your pregnancy standards is something you'll have to decide for yourself, and no one will take you to task for it. But I found my disposition was much improved when I continued to "act pregnant" and be on my best behavior.

There wasn't much I could give Emily during her time with us. But maybe I could give her good nutrition and make sure her birth wouldn't be accompanied by a caffeine-withdrawal headache.

GUILT

Guilt. It's insidious, isn't it? If we felt guilt for the things that actually caused our children's disorders, these are the things we would be saying:
- There shouldn't have been those weird chemicals in the environment.
- It's my fault the chromosomes divided improperly.
- I can't believe I didn't do more to close her neural tube.

It sounds kind of silly when we put that way. Instead, what I've heard were parents saying these things:
- I wish I hadn't polished my nails.
- It must have happened because I'm a bad mother.
- God is punishing me because I did something immoral when I was seventeen.

We're being illogical when we fall into this trap, of course. There's nothing you could have done to guarantee a healthy pregnancy and a healthy baby. If there was, you'd have done it.

A lot of times, we feel guilt that doesn't help us. My stepfather tells me the only thing we need to feel guilty for is sin, and I think he has a point. Guilt is useful if it causes us to right a wrong. By the time we end up reading a book like this, the problem can't be righted any longer, and you did no wrong because, as I said before, no parent deliberately caused his or her child's birth defect.

Guilt is our way of taking control over a situation we can't control. I thought that if only I could find a way I was responsible for my daughter's birth defect, then I could completely eliminate the risk of it happening again. We could resolve to be more careful about teratogens in the future. I wouldn't polish my nails, and I wouldn't let my kid watch as much TV. I would thereby ensure perfect pregnancies.

It's an illusion. We can't change accidental exposures or take ourselves back in time and make our baby's chromosomes line up correctly.

We can try to wear guilt like armor against the pain, but like actual armor, it's going to weigh us down. We need to let that go, but I think in some respects that means opening ourselves up to a worse feeling: that of helplessness.

ANGER

Guilt protects us from helplessness in part by making us good and angry at the evil person who caused our baby's condition. (Ourselves.) Sometimes, though, we direct that anger outward.

I was unreasonably angry on the drive home after the diagnosis. I passed an auto body shop where someone was welding. How could somebody be welding? My world had just ended.

Now arguably, parents in our position should feel enraged. All manner of people have polluted our environment to make an extra dollar, and some corporations hide icky chemicals in foods because colorful shelf-stable food earns them more money.

You could be angry at a spouse who wanted to have a baby even though you didn't (or didn't want to have the baby and wasn't enthusiastic enough).

You can be angry at the medical staff who aren't very forthright or gentle about giving us the answers we need.

Oh, and the big target: there's God, who we all know is perfectly capable of giving us a healthy baby. (We'll talk more about that later.)

Anger is perfectly understandable, but I'm not sure it's helpful. Chronic anger is a shield, like guilt, but it's going to insulate you from the pain at the cost of also insulating you from really connecting with your baby.

I have no quick tips for this one. All I could do was tell myself that right now I needed to be concentrating my energies on my baby and all the planning and bonding I'd have to squeeze into the remainder of the pregnancy. It's not that much time.

GALLOWS HUMOR

This was how I coped. My Patient Husband and I have a similar sense of humor, but I get very dark, biting, and sarcastic under stress. I've always said that if I can laugh at something, I can get through it, but it turns out some of those laughs are really hard-won. Seventeen years later, I don't think I've ever laughed about Emily's death. I've laughed about a lot of the circumstances surrounding it, and I've had plenty of good laughs at my own expense (I hope by this point you have too) but about her death, I just can't. And that's okay.

If you find yourself coping with sardonic laughter, that's fine. But keep in mind how others will respond: they won't be sure whether to laugh or scream. They might urge you not to say such things. They'll get that look you'll eventually come to recognize as the "deer in the headlights" expression: eyes wide, face carefully blank.

It's fine to get a dark laugh or two out of the worst thing you can imagine happening in your life. Just screen the company in which you do it.

TIPS: BONDING WITH YOUR BABY

You're doing this for the sake of your baby. You wouldn't carry around an infected appendix for four more months, after all. But it's very hard to build a relationship with someone you can't see and who really doesn't respond much to you. Some women get the diagnosis even before feeling the baby kick. Fathers never get to feel their baby's kick from inside their own bodies. So how can you bond? There are many ways. Not every suggestion will be for everybody, of course, and you will probably find ways I never mention. What's important is that you establish the bond, not the specific way you do it.

JOURNAL

I have kept a journal from time to time all my life, sometimes for specific purposes (e.g., a spiritual journal or an artistic journal). They're great for capturing those moments you don't want to forget, and anyhow, I'm a writer. What else am I going to do when I have all these huge feelings and nowhere to put them?

About a month after the diagnosis, I dug out an old notebook and began writing letters to Emily. I didn't intend it, but this ended up creating an image of her in my head. When you're writing letters, you're in a way anticipating the responses of the person on the other end. So while you can claim it was mostly imagination (bolstered by just a hint of actual data) it was a way of bonding with her.

Plus, journaling was therapeutic. What you write in a journal you don't need to scream at the doctor. Or at the clueless neighbor. Or at your spouse.

Even better: writing in a journal is subversive. On days when you don't feel like dealing with anyone, take out your journal and start writing because they'll avoid you. Why? You could be writing anything in there. By instinct, they stay away.

I journaled so often that my toddler, on finding my notebook unattended one day, decided to do what I was doing. There he was, scribbling all over a blank page near the back, and he agreed that he was writing a letter to Emily too.

My husband also has a journal he writes in from time to time, but he used it more to record the prominent events than to bond with Emily. (He's an engineer. He collects and preserves data.) That's fine too. We'll appreciate having that in future years as the memories get fuzzy.

POETRY

I wrote a bunch of poems to and about Emily. I'm not sure how good they are, although some of them got published in magazines. (That's the thing about poetry: you never really know if it's any good because there's so much interpretation.)

I've seen poems on many memorial web sites: poems to the baby, for the baby, about the baby, poems by both father and mother, poems from the baby's point of view. If you think it might help, give it a shot!

If you protest that you're not a poet, remember that it doesn't have to be excellent poetry. (Gosh, please go back and forget everything your scowling English teacher said in junior high school. Yes, lots of poems are awful. Yours won't be because it will be *yours*. Leave the Nobel Prize in literature to other people, and you just work on getting through this time in your life.)

First and foremost, the poem would be a tool for you to get in contact with your baby. If it accomplishes that, then it's a success. No one else ever has to see it, and if you find you're truly embarrassed, you never have to admit you wrote it. But don't sell yourself short. Try writing a poem and you might be pleasantly surprised!

If you can't deal with writing your own poems, you might find other people's poetry helps too. Poetry accesses a less rational part of the brain and allows you to connect more directly with images and feelings by using your inductive logic. See? That almost makes it sound good for you, so don't rule it out.

MUSIC

This was huge for me. You think poetry accesses those emotional parts of the brain? Move over, poetry. Let's try setting you to music.

The weekend after the diagnosis, I started learning guitar so Emily would hear some music during her lifetime. My mother brought me her acoustic guitar and my friend came over to show me some chords. I sat in the living room with the *Glory & Praise* book and one chord at a time would stumble through the songs we heard at church every Sunday.

Because the guitar presses right up against the belly, I figured Emily was sure to hear something. They said she'd be deaf, but the vibrations should carry through the amniotic fluid.

I taught myself for a couple of months, singing along with the chords. Singing to her sometimes, to myself at others. I'm afraid it might have backfired, though. See, the best thing you can say about my guitar playing is that it drowns out my singing. Between that and the children's choir Emily heard at church every week, maybe God asked everyone to keep it a secret from her that there was music in heaven, at least for the first few weeks. (Poor kid.)

When I was pregnant with my first child, whenever I sang, imagined myself singing to him. I was able to do this with Emily as well, although not as often with her. My heart just wasn't in it.

One way I used music, though, was to compile a tape of songs that made me think about Emily. I listened to that tape several times during the pregnancy, during labor, and a few times after she died. (Later on, in the age of iTunes, I transferred it all to a playlist, and I listen to it on her birthday.)

Listening to those songs made me feel closer to her, even though a few of them make me bawl. After her death, at times when I felt I needed a good cry but just wasn't able to, I'd pull out the tape and listen. It gave me permission to just let go. Sometimes I hear those songs on the radio, and they're a built-in trigger for me to remember Emily at times when I might be thinking about regular life. They keep her memory vibrant for me.

(And then there are the...well, spooky times. Once a couple years afterward I was thinking about her and aching for her, and then, on the radio for the first and only time in seventeen years, came the one mega-Emily song that I think of as hers, absolutely hers. Do you think she asked God to send me a little spiritual kiss with that song?)

CATCH PHRASE

I was told Emily would be deaf. (This was, in fact, something the doctors seemed to think was a slam-dunk reason for me to abort the pregnancy: "She'll be deaf and blind." And when I remember that, I think, *Helen Keller?* Of course someone can contribute to the world while deaf and blind.)

Regardless, I believe the doctors were wrong: she got very still whenever there were loud noises. She stilled for my voice; maybe that was vibration and not sound?

But she stilled when my husband spoke or when my son yelled at my belly. Once when something fell with a loud bang, she jumped!

So much for medical knowledge. I've since learned of other anencephalics who were receptive to auditory stimulation, even if it isn't "hearing" the way most people understand it. So in my opinion, every parent ought to consider using a catch phrase with the baby, even if told the baby is deaf.

Our "catch phrase" started as a game. Any time Emily stuck her feet up into my rib cage, I'd rub on the lump of feet jutting out from my side and say, "Silly feet!" I always said it the same high-pitched voice, and I always did it while touching her feet, which she would then withdraw.

Who knows if Emily even noticed, right? Even a healthy newborn might not make the connection.

My toddler loved "silly feet." He used to rub my side and say, "Emily has silly feet!" One day, he'd even rubbed his own side and exclaimed, "Silly feet!"

So that night, I related to my husband how our son had said "Silly feet!" and I used the right tone of voice, too.

As soon as I said it, Emily stuck her feet up into my ribs.

I was stunned. Did she really respond to my voice? And not just to my voice, but to specific words? So I rubbed her feet, which she quickly pulled away.

After her birth, holding her, I said, "Silly feet!" She opened one eye and moved her head toward me.

Yeah. I'm sure she knew it was me.

In subsequent pregnancies, I tried this again with a different phrase, and the babies responded in similar ways. So I suggest trying, on the grounds that it can't hurt and it might help.

HEARTBEAT

I bought a heartbeat monitor at Toys R Us for $20. It wasn't a Doppler monitor like the ones your doctor or midwife uses, but just an amplified stethoscope.

Did it work? A bit. I was able to locate Emily's heartbeat on one try out of four, more often after I learned how to gauge her position by manually palpating my uterus. When we did find her heartbeat, we found it incredibly comforting to lie back and listen. That was the sound of life and the sound of steadiness.

Toward the end of the pregnancy, when she engaged and faced my right side, I couldn't detect her heartbeat any longer. Unfortunately, I wasn't able to get ahold of a tape recorder until that point. Just before the end of the pregnancy, she turned left-facing for one evening. I managed to set up the monitor and the tape machine and capture her heartbeat on tape before she turned back to face my right side again. I felt as though that was a gift from Emily to me.

In the intervening seventeen years, other sound-capturing methods have worked to get that sound digitized, and someone even told me the boutique personalized bear shop at your local mall has a way of capturing the heartbeat so you can put that into one of their fabulously expensive bears. I pass along that information without any knowledge of whether it's true, but it might be something to look into.

PERSONALITY

No one can convince me that babies are blank slates whom we program with personalities as they grow up. Newborns can have distinct personalities. Why not babies in utero too?

The character traits I guessed about my firstborn based on his pre-birth behavior actually turned out to be fairly accurate. When I rolled over in bed, he'd kick me until I rolled back to the position he preferred; he's still single-minded and dislikes change.

I paid attention to the things Emily did in the hopes of getting a sense of her personality. Amazingly to me, she did seem to have a personality, and rather a strong one. She had preferences about being touched, the kinds of sounds she wanted to hear, and what position I should lie in to fall asleep. Good heavens, was she just as stubborn as her brother?

She was a fighter, and that was borne out by how she struggled to hang on after her birth. I wondered then, as I have frequently wondered since, if she had a personality and the doctors say she had "no brain" (or rather a very underformed one), then where is the personality formed?

For more on this question—and not philosophy, actual science—I cite an article from hydranencephaly.com in the links section at the back. A team studied children with limited brain function who could distinguish familiar versus unfamiliar people, could interact socially, and even had music preferences.

ART

If you have visual-arts talent (which I don't) you may want to create some kind of artwork or craftwork for your baby.

You can draw or paint pictures to or for your baby. Some parents can do embroidery or cross-stitch. My friend Lisa tells me it's therapeutic to create collages, and all you need are scissors and glue. I knew some who have crocheted or knitted baby blankets for their children. (I was not at the time a knitter or crocheter. I cannot imagine the output if I had been back then.)

All of these are methods of spending time with the baby and thinking about the baby. I've heard some parents say, though, that they had to make two identical baby blankets—one to bury the baby in, and one to keep for themselves as a memory of that time spent together.

Whatever your artistic bent—be it painting, drawing, sculpture, basket-weaving—do try to channel it toward your unborn child. If our creative selves truly are our highest nature, then your child will benefit from the gift of that part of yourself.

TIPS: SPIRITUAL ISSUES

The death of a child forces us to question all of our core beliefs. Our relationship with and understanding of God will change.

I'm writing this section from my perspective as a Christian. I don't know how to write it any other way, but spiritual issues should be included because so many parents rely on or question their belief system (and many do both!) during this time. Your beliefs, your relationship with God, your practices, your understanding of sacred texts—every one of those will come under the microscope of your heart right now.

FAITH VERSUS PLANNING

Is creating a book (or reading a book) about preparing for the death of your child indicative of a lack of faith in God? I don't think so. If true miracles happened as often as we wished they would, they'd be called "commonplaces."

There is absolutely nothing wrong with praying for God to save your child. I never prayed harder for anything in my entire life. I asked everyone I know to pray, and they spread the word to pray as well. We had 750 people (at least) praying for Emily.

I don't doubt the efficacy of prayer. I truly believe all those prayers had an effect on us. God didn't give us our miracle, but that's not to say the prayers were ignored. I felt the power of everyone's support. I had several experiences that showed me God was enduring the waiting and the grief right at our sides.

If you believe in God as an omnipotent being, then you believe God has the power to heal your child. That's a given.

St. Ignatius of Loyola wrote, "Pray as though everything depends on God. Work as though everything depends on you." This became our motto. We prayed for a miracle and planned for a funeral. I don't think there's a magical number or type of prayers that can force God's hand. There is no correct amount of faith that will coerce God into a healing that isn't in the divine plan. We can ask. We can beg. But in the end, God has the final say.

And that brings us to a very, very important point.

WHAT FAITH IS NOT

I need you to take a look at a jar of poison in my hand. It's a pretty little jar, cut crystal that catches the light. Inside is a golden liquid. It's gorgeous and clean, and it looks tasty. It is destructive.

This poison is a set of beliefs I'd like to call Magical Thinking. There are other terms for it, but I don't want to associate it with any specific Christian belief system because this belief isn't really Christian. When you hear it, it goes like this:

"If you believe enough, your child will be healed."

Look at that. Look at that jar of poison.

The speaker has just handed you a heresy in a beautiful bottle. If you believe, the very act of your belief will coerce God's actions. God will have no choice in the matter but to give you exactly what you demand. Just pretend the healing has already taken place and admit no doubts whatsoever, and *healing must occur*.

Do you see how this makes God less than God?

Do you see how unfair it is to you, the parent? The speaker has just said that if your baby dies, it's your fault for not having enough faith.

The speaker actually believes that you, dear parent, should just pump enough Faith Coins into the Divine Vending Machine, and then push the button marked Healing. The coils of the machine will turn, and your can of Healing will drop into the dispenser slot. Then you can simply reach in and take the reward you've earned.

Oh, pretty little poison that relieves the speaker of any need to empathize with you and denies you any comfort whatsoever. Some women on the support group even reported that friends and family have cut them off because the baby's death proved their lack of faith, or who pretend the baby never existed. How can that be right?

This is not how God works. This is not how a *relationship* with God works. This is not how faith works.

Tell them faith is not a video game, where once you level up your faith score, nothing bad can happen. Tell them that

Jesus said you had to take up your cross and follow Him, not that you could just engage in some bizarre work of "faithing away" all your troubles.

God gave you this baby, however this baby is. Your job is to love your baby.

We read in the Gospel of Mark that Jesus couldn't perform miracles in his home town. It's not because failed to believe hard enough to force Him to work miracles. It's because those people lacked even the faith that He *could* do it. They were, in a sense, ridiculing God.

Isn't making God less than God also a type of ridicule?

I don't endorse ridicule even under the best of circumstances. God most certainly could transform any of our babies into perfectly healthy babies. I believe God could raise my daughter from the dead and heal her even now, seventeen years later. Will God do that? Probably not. That doesn't mean my faith is lacking. It means I have trust and humility, a gift God has probably given to you too.

ANGER AT GOD

The first thing my parish priest said to me was, "Get angry at God. God can take it."

I'm no stranger to anger at God. When my husband contracted cancer back before we were married, I got so angry at God that I couldn't really pray for two years. I felt the anger and either denied it or else waited for it to go away on its own.

It didn't, of course. I felt God had played dirty with me in the way things unfolded, and I lost trust in Him. A year later, my husband's cancer was cured, but my anger wasn't. (I've written out that whole story elsewhere, so I won't bother you with it here.)

It is damaging to any relationship to deny genuine anger. Denied anger is acid, and it can't be contained forever. It dissolves its way out of any container you pour it into, eating through the walls of its jar until it's out, and when it pours out, it scalds you and scalds the person you're angry at, scalds the bystanders, and leaves everyone more damaged than if you'd just admitted to it in the beginning.

Healthy anger is a signal that your boundaries have been violated. Unhealthy anger is a reactive response to pain. God can handle both of them, but God will wait for you to bring it to Him first. Before the cure, you have to admit to the pain.

As you would do with a spouse or a close friend, when you become angry at God, talk it through. I count it as a sign of respect and trust when a friend confronts me about something I did, so I would hope God does too.

A long time ago I read, "Animosity toward God is still contact with God." I believe that's true. As long as you don't cut ties, you can work through the anger and your sense of betrayal in the relationship. Over time you can reach a new understanding.

HOW COULD GOD DO THIS TO US?

So what are we angry about? We're angry about this: that we tried our best, and now here we're going to lose our much-loved baby through no fault of our own. (At least, no reasonable fault—as you saw in the Guilt section, some of us can find many, many faults that caused the problem, such as switching shampoo brands right around the time of conception.)

This question is the Book of Job in a nutshell, and I found a sideways comfort in how the writer of the Book of Job didn't seem to have an answer either.

Thomas Aquinas admitted that innocent suffering is a very good argument against the existence of God. Philosophers and scholars have debated this for ages without reaching a satisfactory conclusion, so I won't even try to answer it here.

I don't know what God has in mind. I know several people tried to tell me that *they* knew what God had in mind, but it didn't help. (But now I know who to ask the next time I need to know the mind of God! I'm sure you've been similarly blessed with those people.)

The conclusion I reached was essentially this: "Children are a gift from God." Emily, anencephaly and all, is a gift from God. I'm not sure why I couldn't keep my gift, but that conviction only grew stronger the longer I carried her.

Emily made me understand the preciousness of time and the precariousness of life. I grew to love her individual soul and what I could decipher of her personality. She has changed me and my husband and our relationship to one another and to the world. She has affected the life of her older brother, and in some ways I believe she's also affected the lives of the siblings who came afterward. She has inspired many and shown others the value of a life, even if brief.

YOUR PRAYER LIFE

Go ahead and guess what my prayer was for five months straight. No, wait, really—go on and guess!

Now the interesting thing here isn't that I prayed for Emily to be born alive, but rather that I kind of felt the whole time that my prayer wouldn't be answered with, "Okay, sure!"

I didn't give up. I knew that much. I knew you were supposed to keep knocking, like the relentless widow that Jesus talked about who insisted the judge should make a ruling in her favor. Every so often I'd cite Scripture back to God (in case He forgot?) about what father would give his son a stone if he asked for bread. Hmm? Well?

My relationship with God back then, while steady, wasn't the greatest. I related to God as if He were CEO of God, Incorporated, an impersonal organization where I happened to be one of the minimum wage underlings. If I were to approach the CEO, I ought to have not just a problem but also a solution that I was requesting permission to enact. I was a good corporate drone. I expected that whatever my CEO had sent down the management chain to me was important for The Kingdom of God, Inc, and while I could appeal, it would probably be denied on appeal.

This is not (in case you were wondering) a healthy relationship to God. A very wise friend eventually pointed out what I was doing and helped me get my relationship to God back in a good place.

However, given my erroneous God, Incorporated mindset, you can see how I came up with the next nefarious plan. In the Catholic Church, to become a saint you need to have first lived a life of heroic virtue, and secondly, after your death, you need to have two documented miracles. The first miracle is for your beatification and the second is for your canonization.

Hmm.

My husband called what happened next "Mercenary Catholicism." I picked out a person who was under consideration for sainthood, and I prayed with a modest proposal: we had a case that was 100% documented and 100% fatal. I offered that I would learn about him and pray and would work for his canonization if in return he would pray for a miracle for our daughter.

(The pre-Saint I picked out was Venerable Archbishop Fulton J. Sheen, and it will not surprise you that the Venerable Archbishop Fulton J. Sheen appears, in the long run, to have wanted nothing to do with me.)

If you're Protestant and you're horrified (or if you're Catholic and you're having a good laugh at my expense), let me just say now that I know this was wrong, and I know why it was wrong. Prayer is not about extracting from God the prize we want. Prayer is the development of a relationship.

That's what prayer is for. It's not just, "Hey, God, gimmee!" Prayer is about reaching out, touching, gazing, adoring, and spending time with God. Prayer is about listening. Prayer is about being together. Imagine if you will Jesus standing in front of me, looking shocked, saying, "I am not your hired gun."

This is where I'd gotten it wrong, and this is where the people who demand total faith in a future healing have also gotten it wrong. Both God, Incorporated and God-Must-Do-What-You-Command miss the point that God is God. He is almighty and eternal, is all-loving and all-knowing, and is very much not under our pathetic control.

Both those mindsets are attempts to reduce God to being less than God. It's less scary to think that God can be controlled if I bring Him my incident report, a plan of action, and even the pen to sign it. Or others want to believe God can be controlled if you just bring an iron-clad statement of faith and never consider any other possibility than that God will do exactly as you specify in your faith-filled command.

Instead, God is huge and marvelous and incomprehensible. We're His children, and fortunately like most parents He knows when we're trying to manipulate Him. Instead He's going to work things out according to a better plan.

What that plan is...? Well, that's where prayer comes in. Real prayer. The kind of prayer where you put your naked soul and wounded spirit into God's hands and trust He's going to be gentle with you, and you ask in all your vulnerability if He can help you understand just a little bit better.

WHAT COMFORTED ME

In the end, it came down to this: I believe that God matches children to the parents best able to love them.

We can answer or ignore this call, and the newspapers too frequently carry stories of parents who failed to love. However, a thought that comforted me and might not comfort anyone else, is that God wanted Emily to exist, and for some reason the Emily God wanted to create had needed us as parents more than we needed a healthy child.

That's what parents do: we sacrifice our *wants* for our children's *needs*. My daughter must, for some reason, have needed me. My peculiar way of loving her must have matched up to her needs better than any other woman. Her father's specific way of fathering her must have met whatever kind of fathering her soul needed.

You will have a certain style of loving your baby too, and that also will best match up to your baby's needs. You are the best parent for your child.

BIBLE VERSES, COURTESY OF MY ASKEW THEOLOGY

You know now that at the time, my theology was a bit askew, so bear this with a grain of salt. Yes, I had Scripture verses that comforted me. They're a reflection of where I was, spiritually, at the time.

Some parents in the support group took comfort in the words God said to Israel right before sending them into exile for seventy years in Babylon, *"For I know the plans I have for you, says the Lord, plans for welfare and not for evil, to give you a future and a hope." (Jer 29:11).*

That's a nice one, and I agree: you're about to endure a whole lot of pain, but there's a reason for it; you're going to benefit in the long run.

But personally, I clung hard to the words of Job 2:10: *"Shall we receive good at the hand of God, and shall we not receive evil?""*

Not that Emily's life was evil, but I needed a much more direct affirmation that God could put me in a difficult situation and that I was meant to be here.

Or this, from Isaiah 45:7:
"I form light and create darkness,
I make weal and create woe,
I am the Lord, who do all these things."

My Biblical history professor, who also taught Biblical Hebrew, says that's a softening of the second line, and that the most accurate translation is more like, "I bring good and create evil." (Which makes sense—Isaiah here is holding the line against Zoroastrian philosophy in Babylon.)

But look at that affirmation there: God created both the good and the bad, the wonders and the struggle. We weren't enwrapped in chaos. Instead we were right there in God's hand, exactly where He wanted us to be. Can a mother forget the baby at her breast and have no compassion on the child she has borne? I couldn't forget my moving little one, and just as I had plans for Emily, God had plans for us.

And look at Isaiah 54:16:
"Behold, I have created the smith
who blows the fire of coals,

*and produces a weapon for its purpose.
I have also created the ravager to destroy;"*

This assures me we weren't abandoned. We were there, being forged by God's tools. Again, while I know most people wouldn't be happy with this, I felt vindicated at least a little.

I don't think I could have handled believing what a number of others told me they thought, that Emily's birth defect wasn't God's doing but rather Satan's. If it was Satan, that makes us a victim. If it was God, that made us and our pain a part of the plan, which we knew had to be a good plan, and I could deal with that.

After Emily's birth and death, when it felt like we were out of the worst of the storm, I eased up a bit on those kinds of verses, and this became very important to me:

"Whoever humbles himself like this child, he is the greatest in the kingdom of heaven. Whoever receives one such child in my name receives me." (Matt 18:5)

I'd always applied that verse to using Natural Family Planning (since we might well end up receiving a child whether we wanted to or not!) but later I saw that we were receiving Emily just as she was. In doing so, maybe we were taking a little bit of Christ into our hearts and our family.

A little further down, Jesus continues, *"See that you do not despise one of these little ones; for I tell you that in heaven their angels always behold the face of my Father who is in heaven" (v 10).*

So many people—doctors, relatives, acquaintances—seemed to despise our babies and then acted as if they despised us. But God clearly treasures our children.

How about this one?

"And the King will answer them, 'Truly, I say to you, as you did it to one of the least of these my brethren, you did it to me.'" (Matt 25:40).

Some people might look on our babies as the least in the world. I even had a therapist opine that Emily wasn't a human being. But Jesus is saying that God is going to accept anything you've done for your little one with the same force as though you did it for Him.

And really, you're just loving your baby. You're doing what any parent would do.

In the sermon at Emily's funeral, the priest spent a long time talking about how two sparrows can be sold for a penny, but not one falls without God's notice (cf. Matt 10:29). God did take note of Emily's life. And God definitely made use of her life on this earth.

BIBLE VERSES, COURTESY OF OTHERS WHO ARE BETTER-BALANCED

You might prefer these, offered up by members of the support group:

> *But now thus says the Lord,*
> *he who created you, O Jacob,*
> *   he who formed you, O Israel:*
> *"Fear not, for I have redeemed you;*

> *I have called you by name, you are mine.*
> *When you pass through the waters I will be with you;*
> *and through the rivers, they shall not overwhelm you;*
> *when you walk through fire you shall not be burned,*
> *and the flame shall not consume you.*
> *For I am the Lord your God,*
> *the Holy One of Israel, your Savior." Isaiah 43: 1b-3a*

"We know that in everything God works for good with those who love him, who are called according to his purpose." Romans 8:28

Monika Jacquier writes:
The first and most important for me :
For this perishable nature must put on the imperishable, and this mortal nature must put on immortality. When the perishable puts on the imperishable, and the mortal puts on immortality, then shall come to pass the saying that is written:
"Death is swallowed up in victory."
"O death, where is thy victory?
O death, where is thy sting?"
The sting of death is sin, and the power of sin is the law. But thanks be to God, who gives us the victory through our Lord Jesus Christ. 1 Corinthians 15:53-57

*God gave me this passage some days after Anouk's diagnosis. Immediately
I decided that it would be on the birth announcement. Even if at this
moment everything seemed lost, I knew through this verse, that it was
only a battle but not the war.*

*"Man looks on the outward appearance, but the Lord looks on the heart" (1 Samuel 16:7) helped me to look at Anouk with my heart, not my intellect. It's not
the lack of her brain who makes her less important in God's eyes.*

Psalm 46.1 was my motto during the last months:

*"God is our refuge and strength,
a very present help in trouble."*

There is also a German proverb I'll translate :

Turn your face towards the sun, so the shadows will fall behind you.

MARY LOST A SON TOO

Although I've been Catholic all my life, I wasn't comfortable with the Virgin Mary. (You've already seen I have plenty of theological issues.) I figured it was good enough to honor her because the Church asked me to, and otherwise, we could have a business relationship. God had set her up for honors, so I would honor her as the Queen

Mum, and that would have to suffice. I didn't really *like* her. She was just…there.

Going through the pregnancy with Emily, I didn't ask Mary for help. I didn't go to Lourdes seeking a miracle (I felt that would have been rude and hypocritical) and I didn't even ask for her intercession.

But afterward, I found myself softening toward her. She lost a Son too.

I sat in a hospital bed and held my daughter while she died. Mary stood at the foot of the cross and watched her Son die. Emily was born into a nurse's hands and laid in my arms. Christ was pulled down from the cross by a soldier's hands and laid in her arms.

It was a point of connection. I began wondering how Mary dealt with the complicated psychology of watching her Child die and then later on getting Him back…and then losing Him again after He ascended into heaven.

Herod's slaughter of the Innocents in Bethlehem was unbearable to think about after Emily's death. I felt like a peeled onion, raw and exposed all over, imagining the grief of a whole city. But what of Mary's grief, knowing all those babies died because Herod was looking for hers?

Did she have PTSD after seeing her Son's body nailed up and left hanging there until dead? Did she do as I did and sometimes sit up in the night in the middle of mentally reenacting a scene she'd much rather have forgotten?

I couldn't look at the Madonna and Child Christmas cards we got that year. But afterward, when I thought of her moving in with John because Jesus had given her to the Church as our Mother…I began to soften up toward her. She had a hard life, and I began to feel like she understood me where I was.

"GOD, SHE'S PREGNANT WITH A DYING BABY."

Years after Emily died, I was at Mass and praying for another mother who was set to deliver. She had a very difficult set of circumstances, and I'd made her a baby blanket, but there's only so much you can do. She was across an ocean from me. All along I kept hearing her reporting conditions that I associated with stillbirths, and now she was having preterm labor. The baby was coming.

On my knees, I prayed for her, begging God to at least let her have time with her little one alive in her arms. I was so upset. This mother, in the middle of her own struggles, had also been very good to me, and I didn't want her not even to have time with her son.

All of a sudden, I felt as though I were in a spotlight, as if someone very important were paying attention to me. I knew, right then, that it was the Holy Spirit talking to me, and that spotlight feeling was as good as saying, "I hear you. I've got this."

I urged God, *She's pregnant with a dying baby.*

In my heart, I heard God's reply: *I'm pregnant with a dying baby too.*

I felt then that this is how God feels about all the human souls who have rejected Him. That we're all encompassed by God, and He gives us everything we have. In so many religions, God is our Father (or our Mother). God is our source, and because we have free will, we can reject Him.

I felt this dazzled connection for just a breath of time: that God's position in regard to souls who would abandon Him is the same as a mother whose baby is dying. There's the love. There's the nurturing. There's giving everything.

God knows our pain as intimately as we do, and He's going through it with us. I took comfort in that, so I'm sharing it here.

The mother in question did deliver that day. Her son was born alive, and I believe she had two days with him, surpassing everyone's expectations.

TIPS: THINGS YOUR BABY NEEDS

You will want to prepare more than just yourself. You'll also need some "stuff," so here's where we go over the prosaic things you might need…and one thing you might not.

DECISIONS

Anencephaly is a very straightforward birth defect. We didn't have to decide whether to have Emily put on life support or to attempt invasive, life-saving surgeries. Some other conditions are like this as well: no question as to how lethal the defect is, and no treatment decisions to be made.

Many parents, however, have to decide whether to take extreme measures in the hope that they might save their child's life. I have no answers, except that I'm not sure there is ever a moral obligation to take extraordinary measures.

Because some situations have no clear-cut answers, it's vital that the parents and the doctors discuss all options and make as many decisions as possible ahead of time. The hospital, the maternity unit, and the pediatric unit can all be prepared in advance for the most likely scenarios. In addition, because you're likely to second-guess your decision no matter what it was, it's best to know you made the decision in a calm state of mind after being fully informed.

Feeding isn't an extreme measure, but I've heard of hospitals withholding food from terminally ill infants. Discuss this in advance, and decide whether you want a feeding tube. If the hospital balks, you can change hospitals easier now than you can afterward.

Of course you should leave some decisions open-ended; unexpected situations or new information may arise that would change your mind. If at the time of the birth, other factors arise that would change your decisions, it's still better to have a starting ground to work from. Moreover, you'll be able to compromise better if each parent knows why the other parent wanted what he or she wanted.

Some parents may have to make the decision about organ donation. This too is best discussed far in advance of actual need. Because some methods of removing the organs may be ethically controversial, find out how the organ donation will be performed, which organs may be donated, and what criteria your doctor will use to determine whether your baby is a suitable donor.

CLOTHING

Buy at least three outfits for your baby. Two are for the hospital. Even if you decide not to dress the baby in either one, you will still treasure them afterward because they belonged to your baby. The third will be for the burial.

In addition, because Emily's anencephaly would profoundly affect her head, I bought some hats. Anencephalics will need very small hats.

Lately I've begun seeing services that can take off parts of a woman's bridal gown and turn them into a burial gown for the baby. I have no idea how to find one of those (Google would be a start, or a local tailor) but the mothers who've had it done were very pleased with the result.

What you choose should be determined by you and not by your friends. My friends tried to push me into buying a frilly pink dress. I hate pink. I don't normally wear dresses. I'm not a frills person. My daughter would probably take after me in at least some of these respects. I also know that her brother was born very dark and blotchy-skinned, and pink wouldn't look good against that complexion. So I bought red outfits, and I was very pleased with this decision. Whatever clothes you decide on, make sure you're happy too.

CAR SEAT

If there is a chance your child will live long enough to travel home, you'll need a car seat. Have one at the ready, either one from an older sibling or ready to borrow. You don't need to install it, but do make sure you know how it attaches and how to safely buckle in your child.

If you want to buy one, safety experts recommend you buy it new. Used car seats might be past their discard-by date or have been in an accident that created stresses in the plastic. A new car seat should still be within its safe dates long enough for a possible future child to use it (if you do end up having future children.)

STUFFED ANIMALS

Ha ha ha, things your baby "needs." Yes, Emily needed this.

I had bought my son a specific stuffed animal, and I ordered an identical one for my daughter in a different color. (If you're curious, it was a Gund Snuffles.) I intended to bury Emily with her bear, and I brought it with us to the hospital.

"You're going to have an important job to do," I explained to the bear, because of course I talk to inanimate objects. "You're going to have to stay with her forever."

The bear was much bigger than I expected because I totally guessed at the size, but it turned out to be just the right shape for me to cradle throughout labor and after Emily died. There's something maternal about needing to have something in your arms. I found myself kissing it on the nose frequently. I missed that bear afterward, and I wished I had bought two of them.

Luckily, one of my relatives had bought Emily a different stuffed animal, and I have that to cuddle when I feel lonely for her. I recommend buying two stuffed animals for this reason. Also, every year when we take our family pictures, we bring that stuffed animal with us and pose it in the photos. People don't ask us why because by now they expect a little lunacy from my family, so it's a kind of stealth memorial.

(Years afterward, in one of those very strange moments that peppers my life, as I was driving, *I saw a Snuffles bear* in a pile of stuffed animals by the side of the road, marked *FREE*. I exclaimed, "I know that face!" and slammed on the brakes. He was the same color as Emily's, and I brought him home. This one was much smaller, so he went onto Emily's memorial shelf.)

PLASTER MOLDS

There are kits that you use to mix an imprint material, and once that hardens, you pour plaster over it and dry it. What you have in the end is a three-dimensional imprint of your child's hands or feet.

A lot of baby boutiques will sell specialty plaster mold kits for lots of money; we got ours in the craft section of Walmart. We bought two, one for hands and one for feet. If I could do it over again, I would have bought three: one to try a test run beforehand.

I also would have brought a measuring cup to the hospital to measure out six ounces of water for the imprint material. We took two molds of her feet because the first didn't come out very well due to the wrong amount of water. (Since the mold will last forever, we waited to pour the plaster over the mold later on at home.)

I'm glad we have the imprints, although initially I was squeamish. As with photographs and video, if you do it and don't like it, you can discard it later, but you'll only have one chance to get it.

BABY BLANKET

A friend who was herself carrying an anencephalic baby was kind enough to crochet a tiny cap and a baby blanket for Emily. We opted not to bury those with her, but rather took them to the hospital with us and have saved them here. It's good to have something soft and cuddly that belonged to Emily.

BABY SLING

If you've never seen a baby sling, it's a long piece of cloth that you wrap around your body and use to carry your baby in a personal hammock. There are several different kinds of these, but I recommend the type that's essentially a long rectangle of cloth with a pair of rings on one end to feed the other end through. This is usually called a ring sling.

Wearing Emily's baby sling before her birth was like putting on a hug. While it was a bit expensive, I justified the cost because it would also work for other babies we might have.

The biggest advantage of a baby sling is that you can wear your baby all day long, even to nurse, and the baby will always be close to you and able to hear your heartbeat. I know that if Emily had lived for several days, I never would have put her down.

On a more prosaic note, should your baby be one of the rare few who live for months, you can put him or her in the sling when you go out. Two benefits: firstly, if your baby requires oxygen, the tank will fit into the sling with him; and secondly, the sling will effectively "hide" your baby from the world.

A normal-size sling swallows up a tiny baby. This was important to me, since Emily's condition was a very obvious one and might turn more than few faces white. If you've had a baby before, you know there's no surer way than a newborn to get people to walk right up to you and take a good look. You may want to spare yourself the pain of shocked faces.

The brand I bought was a Maya Wrap ring sling, the comfort fit style. The "tail" can be be flared out to cover your baby entirely while nursing. (I've also playfully whapped people with the tail to keep them at a distance, and it works.) Also, if your baby falls asleep in it, you can bend over your bed until the baby is lying down, then loosen the ring and slip yourself out of the contraption, leaving the sling over the baby like a blanket. They're at www.MayaWrap.com.

FEEDING

Some conditions leave a baby unable to nurse in the conventional way. I've heard that the Haberman Feeder is very effective in helping babies with neural tube defects or cleft palates. I'm not sure if it's useful with other conditions. In my mind it was a worthy precaution even though we never used ours. Afterward we donated it to a crisis pregnancy center.

Ask your maternity unit how they feed babies who have issues with swallowing. If they provide their own specialized bottles or feeding gadgetry, you might not need to purchase anything.

A PLACE TO PUT IT ALL

You may want to make a memory box. I started out with all Emily's things in a sewing box that was pretty enough to put out on display if I chose to do so. I've since acquired a nicer jewelry box (minus the tray) as a memory box, but I use both. I've heard of others using a small cedar chest.

Some articles went straight into a fireproof box where we keep things like birth certificates because the postpartum-bereaved me was pretty sure everything was going to get lost in the worst way possible. I don't have a problem admitting that's ridiculous, but still, that's where some of Emily's things are stored.

YOU'LL NOTICE WHAT I DIDN'T MENTION

A crib. Here's my opinion, and it's only an opinion, but if you have a limited time with your child, why separate for sleep? You can put your child into your own bed.

Look up the current guidelines for safe co-sleeping, and then follow those. Unless you frequently fall out of bed or are heavily medicated, you won't roll over on him. When moments with one another are so limited, it seems silly to waste eight hours out of every twenty-four in separate rooms.

TIPS: DEALING WITH FAMILY AND FRIENDS

They're going to be your biggest support. In my case, I kept my sanity because of them. At the best of times they're your community, and at the worst of times they'll hurt you worse than any stranger could (which is why all these folks will make a reappearance in the section on Clueless people). It's not easy for you, but it's also not easy for the people who know you.

Before we start, I'm going to introduce you to what I call "Plus One Theory." According to Plus One Theory, which I invented myself because it needed a name, all your relationships will be exactly as they were before—plus one. So if you have a friend who tended to be selfish, she'll still be selfish…plus one. If your mother was overprotective of you, she's going to continue to be overprotective…plus one.

People don't change during a crisis, but they do seem to become the more intense version of themselves. They behave under pressure the same way they always have unless they make a serious effort to change their habits. Keep in mind while dealing with everyone for the next five months that all their normal characteristics are going to be intensified.

And yours are going to be as well. Your relationships could get interesting.

YOUR PARENTS

They're probably among the first people you phoned after getting the news, maybe the actual first.

In a way, I think it's as terrible a blow to the baby's grandparents as it is to the parents. They're not immediately in the situation, but they had their own dreams for your child. Even when you can't cry, you can count on the grandparents to cry for your baby. They will feel the same strain on "breaking the news" to their friends. They might end up in the middle if you need them to spread word through the rest of the family because yourself can't.

At the same time, because your parents know you and don't keep their "guard" up around you, you may find your parents say the most hurtful things of anyone. Several individuals on the support forums said their own mothers came out with by far the cruelest words about the situation.

Forget what I said above about Plus One Theory. I suspect that whatever your relationship to your parents and stepparents is before the diagnosis, you can multiply it by ten, and that's how the relationship will be afterward. During a crisis, people tend to dig in and react the way they have always reacted, but their parental instincts have rallied. An overfunctioning parent is going to overfunction in very high gear, whereas a neglectful parent is going to take up five new hobbies and quite possibly schedule a vacation for your induction date.

Therefore be sure to ask for exactly what you need. Don't be afraid to shake up familiar interactions by making very specific requests. *Dad, I need you to back down a bit on this.* Or, *Mom, please don't schedule a vacation for right around my due date.*

Your parents, step-parents, or foster-parents will go through the same grief stages you do. They might blame themselves (as if they chose the genes they passed down). They might blame you. They might get depressed, go into shock, and/or want consoling from you.

On top of that, because you're *their* child, many grandparents have seemed to want to step in and take the pain away. They can't, of course. But they want to. They kissed it and made it better when you were three, and now…well, they can kiss it, but they can't make it better.

Theirs is a dual pain: they hurt for their child and their grandchild at the same time. If children represent the future, I think grandchildren may do that even more.

I wasn't as thorough as I could have been with my parents. It never occurred to me that I ought to be passing along all the information I got at the time I got it. My mother conducted her own internet search and came across much of the same information I did (including the same shock photographs); my father waited about a month and then did the same, and although he seemed to avoid the terrible photos, he was still very upset. I should have prepared both of them for the stories they would find online.

My parents-in-law didn't do any kind of internet search, and it's my fault that they didn't have as good a grasp of anencephaly and what it would mean. They had never seen a photograph of an anencephalic, and while I don't agree with Dr. Tactless that "these babies look pretty hideous," their appearance can be a bit shocking.

I did keep everyone updated as time went on. After every midwife visit, I would send a "midwife report" to a select group: my husband, my closest friend, my parents, and my parents-in-law. This helped them go through the ups and downs with us. This worked well enough that if you have a means of sending a mass report to those closest to you, it's worth considering. Facebook groups, group emails, or the CaringBridge website are all options to consider.

YOUR SIBLINGS

Siblings are trickier than parents because sibling relationships are incredibly complicated. My husband comes from a rather large family. Of all his siblings, only one ever phoned us after we got the diagnosis, but that's the way their family works. My brother called nearly every week, though, and he and I, while we get along, aren't necessarily close. His calls helped me a lot. Because we grew up together in the same family, he understands my sense of humor. He was forthright that he had no idea what to say and was afraid of saying the wrong thing. But then he never did say the wrong thing after all.

I know other sibling relationships are more contentious. Because you and your siblings are probably in the same stage of life, they may be having babies of their own. They may feel jealous that your baby is getting all the attention (while you feel jealous that they get to keep theirs). They may feel as though their baby is somehow endangered because you happened to lose the genetic lottery with your baby.

In some cases, if your baby's birth defect points to a higher risk for their future children, they may actually blame you. Or they may feel increased pressure because of the mistaken notion that their own children have to "make up" for the loss of yours.

When this kind of sibling struggle arose in one of my support groups, the other women recommended writing a letter to sort through the issues. I would add to that my $.02: just because you write the letter doesn't mean you need to mail it. The act of writing may in and of itself be enough for you to clarify your feelings to yourself. Email or text messaging has got to be the worst possible medium for handling a conversation with high emotions.

YOUR MARRIAGE

YOUR marriage is the single most important relationship during this time, and it's going to be the one under the most pressure. This is the fulcrum. All the pressure points are going to connect here, and this is where all the friction is going to start generating heat.

Even the most solid marriage is going to have difficulties right now, so don't worry if you start noticing problems between you and your spouse. It's not a sign of the end. There's an urban legend that some tremendous percentage of marriages break up after the death of a child, but I've never seen actual statistics that bear this out.

Instead, think of Plus One Theory. Everything is going to go Plus One right now, so small problems will appear major, but at the same time, you're about to be wowed by your spouse's commitment to you and your child.

Most losses hit only one member of a couple. Her mother dies, and her spouse stands in the breech to be strong until she can cope again. He becomes sick, and his spouse takes over until he's doing better. One loses a job and has to find a new job while the other holds up the financials.

But a baby dies and...both are in grief. Both are in shock. Both are in pain.

And they each cope differently.

And at different speeds.

Right. It's just like learning to ride a tandem bicycle with someone who also has never ridden a bicycle before and neither of you has agreed in advance on a place to ride to.

See, if your sibling dies, your spouse isn't affected the same way you are, so your spouse isn't saying, "Gee, you're processing that stage of grief pretty quickly." Or your spouse's godmother is in her final illness, and you aren't thinking, "Why aren't you grieving for her the same way I am?"

But with a baby, each parent unconsciously assumes the other parent is going to go through the same stages of grief at the same time. Or that their spouse will want to deal with the grieving in the same manner.

For example, some people want to talk out their grief. Others want to process in silence. Both are fine methods of coping. When a talker is married to a processor, though, what happens? "She doesn't want to talk about the baby! Doesn't she love our baby?" is going through his head while she's thinking, "For goodness' sake, talking isn't going to fix the baby. Just let me bleed out my heart in peace!"

You can come up with opposite means of coping for every single aspect of the grieving process. Your style of pre-grieving, grieving, processing, healing—your style isn't automatically *better* than your spouse's. It's just your style. But remember Plus One Theory: until you step back, you're going to assume yours is better because that's the way you do things. In addition, if you're the mom, you've got pregnancy hormones reinforcing this belief. Fun times, fun times.

My advice? Be tolerant of differences. Respect your spouse's different methods of handing a crisis. Look for the ways in which your spouse is showing sadness, and learn to gauge his or her moods based on those specific cues.

This baby is both of yours. Yes, some partners will go off the deep end and pretend it's not happening. They need professional help, nothing I can offer in this book. But for regular people who are simply in a situation they never dreamed could happen to anyone and for which they were singularly unprepared, be tolerant of each other. You're each trying to stay sane in a crazy situation.

It's best if you can stay sane together, and that means not attacking one another for taking a different route to the same end.

Don't accuse your partner of not loving the baby just because of a different grief style. Assume the best of your partner. That person you loved enough to make a baby with? Loves you too. Loves your baby. Wants so very desperately to protect you from the hurt you're about to endure and at the same time recognizes that it's impossible.

Your partner is struggling to shield you at a time when your partner can't shield himself or herself.

Your partner is just as helpless as you are.

Your marriage has the opportunity to grow during this time, so let it grow in patience, endurance, and love. Let it grow in understanding. When your spouse does something you would never have dreamed was a rational response for pain, learn why your spouse did it. Listen to what your spouse is saying. Ask for your spouse to listen to you.

My husband's reassurance to me is always, "We'll muddle through." He and I are only barely competent to handle life in the best of times, but we can kind of make it through together.

One of the strangest things about those five months was how my husband and I synchronized our emotions. He left for work before I woke up, so we wouldn't have contact at all some days until he came home at dinner time. And yet between the two of us, we seldom had a "bad day" at exactly the same time.

When I had a truly lousy day, the kind of day where I was crying before ten o'clock in the morning, he'd come home having had a good enough day that he could be strong for me. On a day where I felt kind of almost sort of like we could get through this, he'd come home having had an emotional breakdown at his desk at work, and I could be strong for him.

Some couples have nonverbal signals for one another. My favorite is, *If you come home and the porch light is on, I've had a terrible day*. You might be able to work out something similar with your spouse if you don't want Mrs. Cheerful walking through the door on the day that you're Mr. Dismal.

But overall, my takeaway here is to communicate. You're both in pain right now. Don't bury the misunderstandings. Let each other know when it's getting to be too much so the other can shoulder more of the burden. And do it together. You'll muddle through.

SEXUALITY

Be prepared for any reaction in this area. You may find nothing has changed. You may find nothing works. You'll probably find something in between those two.

If sex is at a crossroads, I suggest that you and your spouse spend a lot of time talking in a non-threatening place and a non-threatening time (specifically, at a time where neither of you is expected to immediately act on what's being discussed). Use a lot of I-feel statements and three-part sentences ("When you X, I feel Y because Z"). Restate what your spouse says to make sure you understood correctly.

You might not even understand your own feelings about sex, and if you've found it hard to talk about it in the past, you may have to talk about it now. Here's one reaction that I've heard: a woman told me once that she and her husband had abstained since the baby's diagnosis and had never resumed sexual relations. Sex reminded her of having conceived the baby. Sex felt to her like it might hurt the baby. Sex after the birth felt dangerous, as though she were courting disaster with another baby who would die. And worst of all, sex felt like treachery: she felt like she was being untrue to the baby who had died by trying to "replace" the baby.

I'm not going to try untangling that for anyone. If you find yourself and your partner struggling with sexuality to that extent, please find a therapist. Sex is wound up in our identities and self-perception, so it's not a shock that the blow of pre-grieving for your baby might throw a wrench into the mechanisms.

Most couples will work it out without needing an outside expert, though, so for now, make sure you're communicating what you want and expect from and for each other. And as I said before: be patient and tolerant.

SO
by Jane Lebak

So strong.

You protect me
when tragedy tears us both.
So sturdy.
On nights when dinner won't cook right
because of the extra salt
my eyes keep adding,
you say it tastes just fine.
So tall.
You stand there
holding me in church
when the hymn cuts my heart.
"It's so hard on your wife,
losing a baby," they tell you.
So disregarded.
You say yes,
She's suffering.
You never admit the same.
So alone.
Sometimes I can't drive. You can.
Sometimes I can't think. You do.
Sometimes I can't stop crying.
But do you ever help me spend the tears?
So shielded.

Our baby has two parents.
One so bowed.
One so firm.

Carrying to Term

Last night I went into the kitchen.
The sound of the dishwater
swallowed my footsteps
as you worked through the pots and pans
I didn't clean because I'm
so tired.
I heard you murmur,
"So sweet.
So small."
I crept back from the door,
so relieved.

Our baby has two parents.
Little one so missed.
Little one so loved.

This poem appeared in the SHARE Newsletter in 2002.

YOUR OTHER CHILDREN

Our son was with us when we went to the ultrasound. He knew something was wrong while we were in the exam room, but he stayed very still and quiet until we were in the doctor's office.

Finally I explained to him that the new baby was sick. My husband gets top honors for what he said next: "We are very glad because we have you, but we are sad because the new baby is sick." Our son never felt jealous of Emily, and I think my husband's gentle reassurance is the reason why.

(My father told me later, "Don't say she's sick because then he might associate regular sickness with dying." Well, yeah, but what was said was said. Sorry, Kiddo. I'm only barely competent at this parenting gig.)

Because we had four months (actually, I went a month overdue so we had five), we took things slowly. We bought books that dealt gently with the concept of death. The best of those was *Nana Upstairs and Nana Downstairs* by Tomie DePaola. We explained to our son that the new baby had a "broken head." We took the advice of those who had been before us and said that Emily did not have all her parts. We reassured our son that he and we had all been born with all our parts.

We used the image of a lightbulb, where sometimes it burns out even though the bulb is still there. Again, not the best image because our son was really literal, and when we planted bulbs the next year, I think he expected something different.

He put it together on his own before we explained that the new baby would die because she had a broken head. He wanted to see a picture of a baby with a broken head. Any time he saw a baby—at the grocery store, in church, at playgroup—he would ask if that baby had a "broken head" or a "fine head."

Our son was able to bond with his sister, and I think he benefitted from that. When he saw me writing in my journal, he wanted to write Emily a letter too. He wanted me to write his name in sidewalk chalk, and then he wanted me to write hers. He came to all my prenatal visits with me. He would listen to her heartbeat on our home heartbeat machine, and one day I caught him in my bedroom with the machine on his stomach, "listening to the heartbeat." Once he gave my tummy a kiss.

Later, when he saw her in the hospital, there was no fear. We offered him the opportunity to hold his sister but didn't press him. He decided he wanted to, and he had the sweetest smile as he looked at her. When he was done, he exclaimed, "I...hold Emily!" He was thrilled.

After she died, we let him say goodbye, and he still had a connection to her. It made it easier for him to understand why I was sad, why we visited the cemetery, why we had all her photographs. Afterward he reassured me that "We will have another baby, and it will not have a broken head," and "If we have another sick baby, I will hold it."

We brought a babysitter to Emily's funeral so that if my son needed to leave, he could. He was great, though. He didn't stay for the graveside service, and that was fine too.

He knew how much he could handle, and we let him participate as much as he wanted.

One night he said to me, "She lost a baby. She had cephaly." Oh yes, little kids listen all the time. That would be why I would urge anyone who wasn't sure, tell your child everything. You'll be the best judge of how much your child is capable of handling at any given time, and on what level you need to explain things. It will be easier for your child if you don't hide the facts. Even a simple explanation is better than none at all.

YOUR FRIENDS

There are two categories of friends: old friends and new friends. The new ones are the friends you made since the diagnosis, networking through other infant-loss support groups. They'll mostly understand what you need, having been there. Very few of those will be Clueless. The old friends are more problematic.

One of my old friends (who remained a friend) commented that the women on one of my support groups were very mercurial. "They get mad if their friends don't say anything, and they get mad if their friends say the wrong thing."

She's right, of course. (She's a special category of friend, by the way—she went through this entire ordeal at my side and even lurked on one of my online groups so she could understand more of what I'm experiencing. That's one in a million.)

Our friends are bound to say or do something that hurts us. Not because they want to be hurtful, but because the whole situation is painful. They'd have a hard time not hurting us.

And us? We have a tendency to lash out when hurt: "You said something insensitive!" Not necessarily. Sometimes they don't do the right thing because there's no right thing to be done.

Case in point? One of my friends delivered a baby girl four weeks after Emily died. The rest of our playgroup was going to have a baby shower for her, and I said that I would buy a gift and drop it off in advance, but I wouldn't attend. They were very understanding of this.

But they sent me an invitation anyhow.

I opened this was totally furious: how dare they! I already said I wasn't going!

My husband and the above-mentioned good friend both said, "You'd have gotten mad if they hadn't sent you an invitation because you'd have said they were acting like you can't handle it."

And the thing that galls me is…my husband and friend were both right. I imagine the baby-shower friends debated whether to send me an invite: should we make her feel excluded by not letting her even know we're having it? Or should we make her feel excluded by reminding her that this woman has a baby and she doesn't?

How would you have handled it? I still have no idea what the right thing would have been. There was no way to win that one.

Do we really want our friends walking on eggshells? They're going to be doing that anyhow. Do we want to give them more reason to fear our friendly fire?

I didn't want anyone to avoid talking about babies in front of me. They had babies; they wanted to talk about them. When they cut themselves short, I felt hurt. But then when they did talk about their babies in front of me, I felt hurt because my baby was dead. This led to the strange twilight zone sensation of wanting everyone around me not to want to talk about their babies. Who was being unreasonable?

I figured this out, fortunately, before making an idiot of myself. Half the time, the trick is figuring out who's actually to blame when we're angry, so I'll pass on this trick I've learned over the years: when *everyone* on earth is aggravating me, what's the common denominator? Yep. It's me. Therefore it's no one's fault, and I need to chill.

"Chilling" is so hard to do when you're bereaved and pregnant, or bereaved and postpartum. I urge you to please try.

Several times I caught myself wanting to cut off all contact with all my friends. (When I wrote the website version of this section, I was still reeling from how a friend of three years turned her face away from me as she walked past that morning. I was debating the merits of calling her up and telling her to go to hell. I decided that wouldn't reassure her of my reasonableness, so instead I wrote a webpage about how to manage awkward friendship issues.)

What I had to do was trust my judgment in clearer-headed times: if they were good friends before, they were probably still good friends now. The biggest issue then became figuring out which problems are theirs and which are mine. When I mentioned Emily and they got a sudden look of horror, that was their problem. If they can't return my wave and feel the need to avert their eyes, that certainly isn't my problem. When they send me an invitation to a baby shower and I'm filled with rage, that's my problem. Try to treat these situations with a generous dollop of good humor.

YOUR PETS

When I came home just after getting the diagnosis, my cat knew before I even walked into the house. Hazel met me at the garage door and didn't leave my side for the rest of the night. She's usually pretty aloof. Not anymore.

For weeks afterward, when I laid down during the day, she'd join me on the bed. She couldn't have understood what was happening, but maybe humans in a state of chaos emit a cloud of dark pheromones. She knew I needed love from someone.

I've heard of other people involving their pets in a different way: making the pet a stand-in for the infant. Cats are usually around the right size to pick up and rock (excluding for the moment my 19-pounder) and although you'll get the Dirty Look of a Lifetime, you can even test out your baby-sling with your cat.

Others have told me their dogs became their constant companions, and I know two people who got a dog as their "new baby."

I don't recommend getting a pet right now. Yes, they're wonderful. Yes, pets help reduce stress, and nothing will ever beat neonatal loss in the high-stress department. But ask yourself how much the flux in your life right now is going to affect the pet. Can you be a consistent disciplinarian for a new dog? Will you keep giving your cat the attention it wants? What will you do when your new betta begins to look a little pale and listless?

When things calm down, you may not want a litter box in the house, or a dog to walk every day. Pets deserve a certain level of care and emotional investment. You'll know your own temperament best and whether you're likely to change your mind, but if you really want to try having a pet now, I have a suggestion: fostering.

Animal shelters are in dire need of fosters for their animals. Fostering is designed to be a short-term investment on the part of the fostering home, and right now maybe you have the time and attention to give to a mother cat who's just had kittens or a dog who's getting over health issues before he can be adopted. If you find you can't handle it, you can give the pet back to the shelter.

And if you find you're in love with the animal and can't live without it, then let me introduce you to the term "foster failure," where the animal's foster home fails to give the animal back to the shelter because they adopt it themselves.

TIPS: DEALING WITH PEOPLE WHO JUST DON'T UNDERSTAND

They're out there. We've all run into them. Once we tell them about our child's diagnosis, there's no predicting what's going to come out of their mouths. They're...the Clueless!

WHO ARE THE CLUELESS?

Let's face it: when it comes to death, we're all clueless. What sets the Clueless apart from the rest of normal society is that in the face of your pain, they don't empathize. They minimize the loss or impending loss. They may tell you your baby isn't human (bad science, there) and it's better she die now than later (I ask for proof on this one).

Most often they'll find platitudes which they will treat as painkillers ("God needed another angel!" which adds bad theology to the bad science). Then, when you aren't immediately filled with joy or relief because they've saved the day with their platitude, they tell you not to be so negative.

The Rude Clueless are actually vindictive, and I hope you won't have many of those to deal with.

Note that many good-hearted people will say something dumb, and anyone who is sensitive will feel as if she has said something dumb, but you'll hear past the fumbling words to the heart.

The defining factor of the Clueless is that they have no heart behind the words. In other words, if you think you're Clueless, you probably aren't.

DOCTORS AND OTHER MEDICAL PROFESSIONALS

ACQUIRING a medical degree doesn't make you correct. I'd like to point out right at the start that I've lost a tremendous amount of respect for doctors and nurses after seeing the way my grandmothers were treated during their dying illnesses and one relative whose doctors should have been arraigned on murder charges. While the care I received during Emily's pregnancy was stellar, I credited that to seeing midwives and not doctors.

However, we're stuck with bodies that get sick from time to time, and that means we need to deal with medical professionals. So, buckle in. And be prepared.

Many doctors coerce their patients into a termination they don't want and don't need. That might be easier for the doctors. It might also be that when faced with a situation like ours, they feel they have to do something. I've heard of doctors who lied to their patients or insulted them because they were carrying to term. Let them be the hero of their own world, and you go find a different doctor. You can search online for a doctor near you with One More Soul, The American Association of Pro-Life Obstetricians and Gynecologists, and The Pro-Life Healthcare Alliance.

It's not always possible. I know on my old health insurance plan, our choice of OBs consisted of precisely one practice. I actually changed health plans in order to escape that cattle car.

If you have an option, do everything in your power to find a supportive professional to take you through the next few months. A doctor or midwife you trust is very important during birth; I've experienced both extremes. I don't say the doctor necessarily has to be caring, but that would help too; I'd rather have a doctor I trusted who didn't care than one who cared but who might try to "look out for my best interests" by manipulating me.

Looking at it from a doctor's perspective, it must be disheartening. All those years of medical school and residency, study and hard work, and your doctor can do nothing to solve your problem. It must be a helpless feeling, and doctors are unused to feeling helpless. Many doctors try to escape that feeling by writing you an antidepressant prescription. All that education, and it's all they can do. Accept the gesture for what it is. At least in that situation, you know the doctor cares.

Your best protection against your own doctor is information. Learn as much as possible about your child's problems and network with other mothers and fathers whose children were affected. Get a second opinion. Ask questions whenever you feel something might not be right. If the doctor wants you to have any kind of procedure, and the doctor has been pressuring you to abort, find out what are the risks that this procedure will trigger labor or end up rupturing your membranes. Yes, I know women whose membranes were stripped without their permission.

But above all, don't stay with a doctor who belittles you and your informed choices. After all, doesn't being "pro-choice" mean that your doctor has to respect your informed choice as much as a choice to terminate?

Here's how a lousy doctor thinks:

TARGET: The patient wants me to solve her problem.

DEFINITION: Her problem is that the baby is going to die.

ERROR: I cannot solve this problem.

RETARGET: Create a new problem.

DEFINITION: Problem is that she is still pregnant.

SOLUTION: End pregnancy.

Your job should not have to be fixing your doctor, but you need to interject in between the ERROR and RETARGET phases. *It is okay if you cannot solve this problem,* you can say. *I'm not asking you to solve this problem. I am asking you to support the pregnancy and respect my decisions.*

A doctor who cannot respect the patient's decisions owes it to the patient to help her find a new doctor.

A WORD OF CAUTION

A nurse wrote to me through my website to say that she didn't know any better when she started her nursing career. That she would pass on platitudes to her grieving patients because it seemed like the best thing to do.

Remember, nurses are trained to solve problems. That's why we have nurses. It's when their training is at odds with what we need that some nurses and doctors run into difficulty.

In some cases, Cluelessness and insensitivity may be due to inexperience and hospital policy. The feeling will be the same as far as you're concerned. You're the one suffering—your job shouldn't be to educate.

But if you have the strength to educate your doctor or nurses, more power to you. Today's insensitive health-care practitioner might be the next Hall-of-Famer, if only she has the courage to really listen to you and the personal strength to change her attitude.

RANDOM STRANGERS

This is the easiest bunch of Clueless people to deal with. Most of them simply don't need to know your baby's diagnosis.

Some of them will need to be told, like the dental hygienist who won't shut up about how much joy you'll have with your little one. Those are easy ones to silence by asking them to change the subject, and if they refuse to change the subject, escalating your insistence at that point.

So you start by being a bit slippery. They ask you if you're having a boy or a girl and you reply with, "I know a family that had five boys. When the mother was pregnant with a sixth baby, she said if it was a girl, she'd have to have a seventh so people didn't think they'd been trying for a girl all that time!" Then follow it up with, "Do you think people really try for one gender over another?" and voila, subject changed.

But let's say they keep dragging it back to you. Then it's time for the firmer, "I'd like to change the subject, please." Why? "Because I'd like to change the subject, please. Tell me about your grandmother's bread recipe." If they keep it up? Oh. I'm bad. I shock people. I will just put it out there as bluntly as I can, and then, at that point, they go silent. Then I feel mean even though I wasn't the one violating boundaries.

It was a dental hygienist who kept pestering me about the newborn I should have had with me. (The anencephaly should have been noted in my chart, by the way.) Eventually she said, "Well is she a good sleeper?" and I said, "She's dead."

That ended the conversation for the duration of that cleaning. But it's not nice, and I shouldn't have done it.

Mildly tougher are the Clueless strangers who aren't really strangers because you have to see them on a regular basis. You don't want to shock and horrify the librarian, the greeters at church, the receptionist in an office you visit frequently, that guy who always is mowing his lawn when you go for a walk... These are people who don't know you and are most apt to throw clichés your way. In most cases it's probably better to just grin and take the dumb things they say because they don't mean it anyhow.

ACQUAINTANCES

Sometimes these people will surprise you. They know you're pregnant and will naturally ask all those pregnancy-related questions. They'll find out afterward when they see you without a baby. But they don't know what to say.

The response I find most memorable was from one woman I'd figured I wouldn't tell at all. One day she started raging about the unfairness of the world and started telling me about a show she saw where a woman was having a wanted baby and it had no brain! I said, "Oh, anencephaly. That's what Emily has." This woman just gaped at me for a very long moment. Then she asked a couple of polite questions, like was I sure. (As if I'd have just guessed at something like this.) At which point she went right back to prattling about her own problems.

The trouble was, I needed to deal with her a few times a week. I could see she really wanted to ask why I wasn't getting rid of the baby, but she didn't.

I say, give them a chance. They'll be surprised when they find out. In their surprise, they'll say something dumb. Maybe it will come from the heart, and you'll have a stronger connection with them. Maybe they'll avoid you and solve the problem of interacting with them. But you may be surprised by some people who suddenly open up and tell you about their sister's loss, or their mother's loss, or something you never knew about them.

In an attempt, they may also suddenly share about their divorce, their deceased pet, or how their computer crashed. You know what? They're trying to give you back vulnerability in exchange for the vulnerability you gave them.

Keep in mind that you are in control of your own information flow. You can choose to disclose or not to disclose. If you choose to disclose, you can choose how much to disclose. If someone wants you to overshare, set nice boundaries and share only what you feel comfortable doing. And if worse comes to worst, you can discontinue the acquaintance.

INTERNET TROLLS

Oh, where to begin?
Block.
Delete.
Don't engage.
Laugh at them.

Internet trolls are the delightful people who like to make other people upset. To them, it's a game. The tools of their trade are insults, blunt questions, fake compassion, and arrogance. These are the people who are trying to spice up their meaningless lives by yammering online about our "zombie babies" and whatnot.

See those above four items in that list? Those are my recommendations for dealing with these booger-eating losers. They thrive on negative emotions, so you need to starve them to death.

Don't try to reform them. That's above your pay grade. Let them go find other prey. Limit your interaction with them to silently praying for them to get a life and maybe to ranting about them with a friend who isn't on the internet.

The last item on the list is laughing at them, and...I'm a bad person, and I've discovered that laughing at these people is actually the worst possible thing you can do to them. They take themselves so darn seriously. But don't do that unless you can engage without getting your own feelings hurt. I suggest waiting about four years after the loss to do that, if then. Keep in mind that as soon as you laugh at them, they will unleash a torrent of anger on you, so I don't recommend it.

And then there are the creepers. I had this one guy email me through my website. He wanted me to know he'd had a dream about Emily Rose, and did I want him to tell me about her. (Recommended course of action: delete this email.) He wrote me a second time to tell me that he'd seen her in a dream, and she was a little baby and was wearing something pink.

By now you know that I was very anti-pink, so I knew this was garbage. The kid sounded distressed, so I wrote to him and said, tell me more. If you have dreams like this a lot, can you tell your mother? Your guidance counselor at school? He wrote me again and said Emily was clutching a doll. Again, she never had a doll, so I knew he was making it up at this point. I replied along the lines of, "Yeah, I don't think that was her, but tell me—do you have a trusted adult you can talk to?" He wrote me back a fourth time, this time to tell me Emily was in a great deal of pain and crying.

Remember, I was years post-loss by this time. I ran a support group. I had seen just about every nastiness the internet had to offer a bereaved mom. Someone deliberately seeking out a bereaved mom to claim her baby was suffering in the afterlife? What a jerkwad.

I warned my support group about what he was trying to do, and I asked them to spread the word as well. And I wrote him again asking him to maybe get some therapy to talk about his disturbing dreams, which were assuredly not about Emily. I also asked my guardian angel to go check out this guy, and after that I never heard from him again.

Cut off the troll's supply of high emotions. If someone contacts you through Facebook to ask why you're making your baby suffer, or accuses you of something worse, just block the person. No need to engage. Total strangers aren't seeking you out and asking obnoxious questions in order to achieve personal enlightenment that they can't find anywhere else. (If they are, they totally should buy this book! But don't engage them even enough to say that. Just block them and snicker to yourself afterward.) You aren't an information charity for the Truly Rude. Guard your emotional energy and your peace of mind instead.

STRATEGIES THAT SHOULD WORK MOST OF THE TIME

Which brings me to the methods I came up with to stop the Clueless from hitting me when I was down.

MENTION YOUR CHILD'S NAME

This is the easiest way to diffuse Cluelessness, at least with the low-level Clueless, the ones who simply haven't thought about your baby as a person.

When talking about the baby, if you know the gender, use it; if you have picked out a name, use it. The woman who sniped at me, "When will it all be over with?" couldn't keep up that nasty tone when I replied, "Emily's due date is July 3rd."

It's refreshing in a way to reply calmly when they ask something particularly rude. "Why aren't you terminating it?" "You mean why am I not terminating Emily?" It gets the point across.

BEING PHILOSOPHICAL

This worked with other people. When I visited the maternity unit ahead of time to ask some questions, the nurse at the desk asked why I was waiting so long to deliver. I said in a very even tone of voice that I probably had 60 more years to live; Emily had five months. Five months wasn't a very long time, considering. She softened up after that.

LYING

Not recommended, but I used this tactic once. A woman I knew from a community organization (and saw a several times a year) said, "And do you have to carry the baby to term?" I said, "Yes," quite honestly, since to be true to myself, I had to carry Emily to term. I just didn't mean it the way she meant it. It ended the conversation, at least until next time.

BEING RUDE RIGHT BACK AT THEM

You shouldn't meet rudeness with rudeness. I know that.

Unfortunately some of the Clueless are also Hostiles. I know several women whose doctors actually used profanity at them because of their decision to carry to term. I only know of one woman who turned it right back at the doctor, so if you don't have a problem with using that sort of language, keep this in mind.

The doctor said something like, "It's not going to change a {profanity} thing!"

The woman shot back, "I beg your {same profanity} pardon?"

It's the beautiful combination of the almost-Victorian formality with the Hostile-Clueless individual's nasty word that really strike the blow there. But you can do it without the little profane zing, too. (Remember Harrison Ford's character in *Clear and Present Danger*? "How dare you, sir?" Perfect.) "I beg your pardon" will, when said coldly, often draw the other person up short. But you can also, if you can keep your temper in the face of the Hostile Clueless, say, "Well, aren't you adorable with your little opinions," and then leave.

Laughing at the Hostile Clueless will be just as effective as laughing at an internet troll, but be warned that this will trigger all sorts of invective at your expense. Only do this if you can laugh even harder the angrier they get.

BEING SILENT

But often, this is the very best response.

There's nothing more menacing than a clearly enraged person who is saying nothing. Look them dead in the eye so they know you are not disengaging. Don't flinch. They're prepared for you to squirm or to have a fight or at the very least give them a chance to feed off your emotions. Deny them that little frisson of victory. And if they're just Clueless, it gives them a chance to think about what exactly they said.

This is a special kind of silence. It's the not-saying that gives the impression of a person coldly burning with fury. If you can pull it off, this works on even the worst Hostiles. Make sure to keep your jaw clenched and a level stare on the individual. Practice in front of a mirror if you must.

CLUELESS FRIENDS

Your friendships are going to change over this. Some will deepen, and some will disintegrate.

If it's strong friendship, it stays strong. Then you know you can count on each other no matter what.

Some friendships will dissolve, and not necessarily because of your friends. Your understanding and your worldview will change as a result of your child's life, and the person who emerges might have different priorities or a different style. Your previous friendships may no longer "fit" the way they used to.

Or, in some cases, you may find you have no more time and energy for someone's drama. I dropped only one friend because of Emily, and I did it because this person's longstanding selfish behavior came to a head. Who has time for that? I came to realize the friendship had always been about her and her needs and her wants, and at a time when I was the one in need, she couldn't see that her self-centeredness was inappropriate. I stopped making contact with her, and she moved on with her life.

Well, bye.

Three months after Emily's death, someone I'd presumed to be a close friend dropped me. That hurt a lot, and it made me wonder who was next. It felt like double-jeopardy, being punished twice for the same "crime." First reality punishes you. Then some friends punish you again by leaving you after you've taken the hit.

I got through that abandonment by counting how many friends had been so awesome to me in the past six months. There were so many people who'd been generous and strong and caring. Compared to that, who did these two selfish people think they were?

Logically, we're better off without friends who are friends of convenience, seeking our company only when we have shining smiley faces. Emotionally, it always hurts to be written off by a friend. No tips here. I wasn't really sure what to do myself.

The majority of my friends pulled low-level avoidance tactics on me right after the diagnosis because they didn't know what to say. I had to seek them out and show them I wasn't scary.

Some talked with me about everything but Emily. I found that they followed my cue for the most part, though. If I showed them I could talk about Emily without breaking into hysterical fits, they relaxed. If I used her name, they used her name. If I indicated that I needed to talk, they'd listen. (I have one friend who would be stunned to know how horrified she looks every time I mention one of my "aberrant behaviors," like visiting the cemetery or remembering my daughter with love. She never says anything about it, but her face telegraphs the tension…or is it fear?)

If you find your friends are distant, they may be following your lead. They may not want to "remind" you, as if you could forget you were pregnant ("Oh! So that's why I'm wearing these funny clothes!") They don't want you to suffer; they don't want to see you suffering when they know there's nothing they can do about it. So let them know what you want (assuming you know yourself what you want).

When they screw up, try to be charitable and keep a good sense of humor. They don't know what to do any more than you do, and their sense of helpless confusion will only get worse after the baby's death.

CLUELESS FAMILY

Family can either be a blessing or a curse (and you'll notice that like friends, they're appearing in two categories). They have the same problems relating to you that friends have, with the downside that you're stuck with them. You can't just cut off your selfish old Aunt Magda who tells you that it's better your baby be dead. It's a lot messier, and inevitably you'll keep dealing with these individuals.

Family members also know you for a long time in most cases, so they assume they know what you're going through. They'll also assume what it is you need or want to hear. They'll share a lot more willingly from their store of philosophical knowledge than even the wisest of the random strangers.

But here's the key: You're family to them and they want to protect you. You'll need to be more charitable than with your friends, but do try to keep things steady with your family. Keep good boundaries and wear your sense of humor like a suit of armor. You don't need extra drama at a time when everything else is getting upended.

STUPID THINGS PEOPLE SAY

People used to give me just the dumbest advice when I had my first child, who was healthy.

Really dumb. Like the guy on the airplane who suggested that I clap my hand over my son's nose and mouth for about a minute to forcibly pop his ears. Right. Advice like that leaves you blinking at the person, unable to decide how to respond at all.

My grandmother had a reply which has served me well, so I pass it along. Ready?

"That's certainly something to think about."

Not that you'll take the advice. Not that you're going to do anything about it. Not that the stupid statement had merit. Just that it's something an individual could, in fact, think about.

As a reply, it's totally neutral-sounding, so the Clueless Individual will walk away happy to know she has solved every problem in your life. Other neutral statements I came up with were "I'll remember that," "I wonder what my doctor would say about that," and "I'll have to tell my husband about it." I think of it as a kind way to tell them off without actually having a fight or causing offense.

PHONES

If someone is being Clueless over the phone, the way to hang up on the person is to hang up on yourself while you're speaking.

If you hang up on yourself mid-sentence, it'll seem like you got randomly disconnected, and you can take a breather until you're calm before letting them get back on the phone with you. It's not a solution, just a mechanism for cooling-down.

If you don't want to hang up on yourself because you think it's rude, you can go for the straightforward approach: "I'm going to hang up now. Bye."

Or you can do what I had one of my characters do in a novel: go to the door and ring your own doorbell. Sorry, gotta go! Someone's at the door. No need to mention the "someone" is yourself.

TIPS: PRACTICAL ISSUES

These are a little miscellaneous in nature, but they're issues you may confront from time to time during the pregnancy. Don't worry if some don't apply to you.

SUPERMAN

Let's play a game of pretend. Pretend Superman exists. He's out minding his own business when a school bus full of kids topples off a bridge, and he catches it. No problem. Then a Buick falls off the bridge, and he catches that too. He starts bringing them back up to the bridge when Spider-Man swings by and says, "Hey, man, can you hold my sandwich?"

He can't do it. Not because he can't hold a sandwich, but because he's run out of hands.

This is what living every day is like when you're grieving (or pre-grieving). You've got both hands full of the weightiest object you've ever carried, and somehow you're supposed to go grocery shopping on top of that? Or pay the bills? Or cook dinner? Or vacuum? How can you be expected to carry on with—or even to care about—all these stupid little minutiae?

Be gentle on yourself. If you find yourself ordering takeout every night for a week, don't worry. Maybe the lawn is tall enough to film *The Oregon Trail*. It doesn't matter. Remember Rule One: Love your baby. Your energies are necessarily diverted elsewhere.

If the chaos and disorganization gets to you, maybe surprise one of those ubiquitous people who says "If there's anything I can do…?" Hand them a sponge and some scouring powder while smiling broadly.

DRIVING WHILE PERMANENTLY DISTRACTED

I will be honest: after we got the diagnosis, I was not fit to drive.

In the office, I'd tried to put my husband's coat on my son. I was not fit to drive, and neither was my husband.

We'd gone to the ultrasound appointment in two separate cars. And yes, we both drove our cars home. A friend gave me a well-deserved yelling-at for that stunt.

I pretended I was driving in blizzard conditions, keeping exactly to the speed limit and about thirty car-lengths between me and the poor souls ahead of me. My husband claims he simply careened home like a maniac.

There were more days I was not fit to drive, and yes, I drove anyhow. But listen to me: it's stupid to drive while impaired. Cars are not toys. We're ricocheting around in these thousand-pound machines while we're blinded by tears or thinking about death, and we're not paying attention.

(I saw someone comment about the driving section of my website, saying, "I wish I'd read that last week. You know, before I backed the car into the closed garage door.")

When you're behind the wheel, repeat this to yourself: "I am driving a car." Right then, you are not a bereaved parent. You are a driver. When the engine's on, the grief needs to go off.

If you're in the same position I was, please consider not driving. If doctor appointments throw you for a loop, maybe a friend can bring you. Maybe it would be worth paying for a car service like Uber or Lyft. There will be some days when the attention drifts, or when you find yourself crying too hard to see. There's no shame in admitting you can't drive on some days. But wrecking your car or hurting someone else because your life is a wreck of its own...that would be a shame. Please be careful.

CONFUSION

It got worse after Emily's death, but it started right after the diagnosis: I couldn't remember things. For one entire week, my Patient Husband asked every day if I could go pick up the dry cleaning.

Him: Can you go get the dry cleaning?
Me: Okay.
That night:
Him: Did you get the dry cleaning?
Me: Oh. No. Sorry.
Him: That's okay.

Me: I'll get it tomorrow.
Next morning:
Him: Could you get the dry cleaning today?
Me: Okay.
That night:
Me: Oh. I'm sorry...

Eventually I asked my Patient Husband to make up a list in the morning before he went to work. It helped, and later I took over list-making duties. I couldn't save the world, but by golly, I could cross "buy milk" off the mighty mighty list.

One day my Patient Husband came home from work to find me sitting at the table writing thank-you notes for the funeral. He walked into the kitchen and scanned it hopefully. I looked up, had one of those "moments of inspiration," and then reached for my list and the pen. Very carefully, I printed, "Make something for dinner."

My Patient Husband said, "So, fast food?"

Speaking of which…

COOKING FOR TWO

Two meals, that is. In the month or two immediately following your baby's birth, there will be days when neither parent feels much like preparing a meal.

In the last month of pregnancy, I found an article about cooking for one month at a time, and I had two thoughts: a) these people must have huge freezers, and b) there's nothing to stop me from cooking two meals at a time and freezing the other half.

I learned that in my case, preparing twice or three times as much food took a lot less time than cooking the same amount of food in separate batches. Meatloaf? Make two. Meatballs? Make twenty-five. (Bake them! Try it. I'm Italian so you can trust me.) Cook a whole chicken and freeze all the leftover meat. You'll be shocked how easy it is to come up with your own "fast food."

Then, after Emily died, all I needed to do was take a pre-cooked meal out of the freezer and get it to an edible temperature somehow. This preparation took a lot of strain off me, and that's why I pass it on.

MAJOR DECISIONS AND OTHER THINGS NOT TO DO

Here's a tip from a friend: "I would add that times of trauma are the worst times to make major life decisions. People tend to do things on the spur of the moment when they are in crisis and then regret them later. Even if these things seem unrelated, it's best to stick to the status quo unless it's either essential (like quitting smoking) or very easily reversible (like deciding to read stacks of trashy romance novels)."

Most grief books say exactly this. While in grief, don't plan to move. Don't decide to quit your job. Don't suddenly realize it's always been your heart's desire to take up cattle ranching. Stick to the rails for whatever it was you'd planned to do before the grief struck.

(The exception would be if your plans were specifically for what you would do while raising your baby; eg, quitting your job to stay home. In that case, it's going to hurt like blazes, but those plans will need to be changed. Still, I suggest staying as close to your old normal as possible while fine-tuning.)

THE PHYSICAL EFFECTS OF STRESS (AKA, WHY YOU SIGH ALL THE TIME NOW)

Everyone reacts differently to stress, and of course this is (we hope) the most stress you'll ever have to handle. Some problems are almost universal in response to stress, though, and I thought I'd make mention of two of them:

• Colds. Many people find their immune system compromised as a result of high stress. Personally, I contracted long-lasting wicked colds two weeks after Emily's diagnosis and two weeks after Emily's death; when I say long-lasting, I mean three to four weeks apiece. If your primary care provider approves of echinacea or zinc or vitamin C tablets, you might consider taking them to build up your resistance. On the non-medical side of things, learn to make a really strong chicken soup (and freeze half of it!). You'll thank yourself later.

• Teeth-clenching. This one's a doozy. Some people tend to clench their jaws under stress, creating massive headaches, neck cramps, tooth pain, and stress fractures in the tooth enamel. I always could gauge my stress levels by how much my face hurt when I woke up in the morning. (Or when I'd relax my facial muscles and feel myself stop snarling…and then relax it again…and then relax it further…wait, was there still tension?) You don't want to require dental work now. Just being aware that you might be prone to clenching your jaw helps you stop it before it hurts you. As a plus, learning to relax the jaw muscles theoretically helps a woman relax the perineal muscles during childbirth. (Aim for the attractive look known as "camel cheeks." It does help.)

This one isn't a problem, but grieving people sigh. Maybe it has something to do with oxygen transfer. Maybe in stressful situations we're not taking in as much air as we normally do. If it happens more frequently than it used to, try to take it as an assurance that you're still fighting. Years later, I still sigh more often than I did.

HOBBIES

One of the support websites I found early on said that you should keep current on all your hobbies. I thought they were kidding, but I did it anyhow. I was glad I did.

I didn't tell most of the other people in my fandom about Emily's diagnosis. Some of them didn't even know I was pregnant. But it helped to have a part of my life that was "normal" (or as normal as I can be) where people didn't treat me like a fragile teacup who might burst into tears at any second.

I also started a new hobby, playing guitar, and found I was able to channel some of the pain into learning. Guitar lessons at the time cost $15 for half an hour a week; a therapist would charge me $70 at a minimum, and I wouldn't have a useful skill at the end of it. (In the spirit of full disclosure, my guitar-playing never really became "useful" per se.)

One of the things I really liked about the guitar was how the instrument pressed right against my abdomen. Emily would have music in her life. If she couldn't hear the music (and really, it was terrible music) at least she could feel the vibrations. And when one of my friends played for Emily's funeral, the guitar she used was my own.

SHOPPING

Grocery stores and shopping malls seemed to be baby-havens when you're pregnant with a dying baby (whereas you can't remember seeing a pregnant woman or a stroller before).

Moms with kids tend to do their shopping during school hours, when the older kids are occupied. You're less likely to see the babies-on-parade if you shop during dinner hour or in the evening. Also about shopping: you're guaranteed not to see babies if you order online!

Note that if you do online shopping for your baby, you're probably going to get ads for baby things. I've been told that Chrome has an "incognito mode" that will prevent your browser from getting loaded with cookies, and therefore prevent this. You could also try resetting your browser or even using an entirely different browser whenever you want to order something related to the baby.

SUDDEN REMINDERS

Little unexpected details may set you off and bring the whole situation to the surface. By their very nature, these can't be prepared for.

For me, it happened one day while grocery shopping as I reached for the milk: I realized the dairy products were going to expire after my daughter did.

Little reminders are in some ways worse than the big ones. You can steel yourself for a visit to cousin Thelma and her newborn. You can't steel yourself for every aisle of the grocery store, every shop in the mall, every headline in the paper... I finally gave myself permission to cry or just feel rotten. Your baby is a part of your life, and it's a testament to your parenting that you've woven your baby into every part of it. Yes, this is one more unfairness in a gut-wrenching situation, but it's part and parcel of who we are as mothers and fathers.

TIPS: THE BIRTH AND BIRTH PLANS

After all your careful preparation, the day finally arrives. It's going to pass too quickly and too slowly, much as the pregnancy has passed. Your chief concern on the day should be your baby, but also on the future: you will want to minimize your regrets and you will want to remember as much as possible. How to accomplish this will differ for every set of parents, but I offer the following thoughts...

HAVE A BIRTH PLAN

A birth plan doesn't mean you're scripting the action, and those who think they can script even an ordinary, low-risk birth are laughably naive. (I can say this because I used to be laughably naive. We won't discuss my first birth experience.)

Some prefer to call it a wish list. In our cases, what we're trying to do is create a best-case scenario for what is already a worst-case scenario. Whatever you want, ask for it. In many cases the hospital will already be providing the things you want. In other cases, they may just be waiting for the patient to state a preference. And if there's something you really want that the hospital will refuse to do, it's best to know that as early as possible.

I've had doctors who told me you don't need a birth plan. Write it anyhow and get your doctor to sign off on it. Keep a doctor-signed copy, and bring it with you to the birth. If you note that I'm a bit combative in this section, see above about "my first birth experience." Hospitals like smoothly running systems where everything is identical, but your experience can't be identical to everyone else's because your situation is radically different.

Every mother ought to have an idea of the type of birth she wants and why she would choose certain options over others. The best kind of birth plan would be useful as a guideline for the doctor or midwife in the case of an unexpected situation where more than one approach is possible. If your general preferences are understood, the doctors can act with this in mind. Of course, if you have stated that you don't want a cesarean but your life would be in jeopardy without one, expect to have a cesarean. Your birth attendant should make medically responsible decisions. However, your birth plan can be a paper-advocate for your wishes at a time when you may not be able to advocate for yourself.

When I wrote my birth plan, I tried not to dictate too much (except for issues I would not relent on, like rooming-in). I explained my reasons for wanting certain procedures and not wanting others; I tried to phrase it as "we would prefer" rather than "you will," and this was well-received by the midwives. They all looked it over in the seventh month, sent me home with edits, and then I returned with a final version. I made sure a copy was on file with the hospital, a few copies in my medical records with the midwives, one on my person, and two in my suitcase for the hospital. Yes, I am overly cautious, but being the suspicious sort, I didn't trust the hospital that had so mismanaged my first delivery to keep track of a single piece of paper. (They never managed to actually keep track of the permission forms I signed, for example. And they wanted those.) My birth plan was important to me; it was not so important to them.

What sort of things ought to be covered in a birth plan? Anything you feel you couldn't live without, of course. But you also might want to mention what measures of pain relief you will consider (and in what order); whether you want your partner with you in case of a c-section; if you would rather tear than have an episiotomy or vice-versa.

As the parent of a baby who may not survive the birth, you also have a second set of considerations:

- whether you want extraordinary measures to prolong the baby's life
- whether you want a chance to hold the baby in the case of a stillbirth *(here's my biased opinion: YES, you do. Don't let anyone tell you it's abnormal to want to hold your baby under any circumstances.)*
- that you want to delay routine procedures until after you've held your baby

- what decisions you've made for the baby's nutritional needs
- what assistance you require in gathering mementos and taking pictures

Demand rooming-in. If you decide later to place your baby in the nursery, that's fine, but make sure the baby isn't whisked away because of 1950s hospital policy. Call as many doctors as you must to secure this right. It wasn't until I contacted my son's pediatrician that I finally found a doctor who would use her authority to say, "They damn well better let her stay in the room with you! If they don't, tell them to call me—immediately! Even if it's two in the morning!" (That's practically verbatim. I loved my son's pediatrician.) Once she took that stand, everyone else behaved.

In writing your birth plan, try to keep it on two pages. Short paragraphs/sentences that get right to the point are good. Elaborate graphics are not recommended. Neither are elaborate fonts. Consider it a medical document which may need to be referenced in a hurry without a lot of distractions.

C-SECTION

Elective surgical birth is a very touchy subject. Some mothers feel their baby has a better chance of being born alive by cesarean than by vaginal delivery. You'll have to discuss this with your doctor, since obviously it requires your doctor's cooperation. So during a regular visit, ask if the method of delivery will raise your child's chance of a live birth.

If your doctor objects to *discussing* a c-section on the grounds that "the baby will die anyhow," you have the right to fight him/her. It matters to you whether your baby is born alive. Therefore you have the right to discuss it.

If you're willing to endure the longer recovery period, what right does the doctor have to say you really don't want a c-section? Offer to sign waivers. Explain that you know the risks, and explain that it will be a lot easier for your emotional recovery if the baby is born alive and lives for even a short while in your arms.

You will want to discuss with your doctor how the recovery experience is different after a c-section, and you will want to discuss how a surgical birth this time will impact any future pregnancies and deliveries. Ask about the potential increase in risk for placenta accreta, etc. Cesarean sections are wonderful procedures that save the lives of mothers and babies, but they aren't risk-free.

(If you previously had a c-section and would like a VBAC this time, open that discussion as well.)

You'll have to take into account previous deliveries and how many more children you expect to have. It's best to get this resolved right up front so there are no regrets later.

One surprising thing we discovered on the support group was that a c-section was not a guarantee of a live birth. You'll want to find out what the statistics are for your baby's specific condition broken down by different methods of delivery.

There's a lot to juggle here. If your doctor won't cover all this during an office visit, see if you can get a separate appointment just to talk about the birth so you can have all your questions answered.

THE BIRTH CENTER

If you can, tour the birth center first and try to speak to the director of the maternity unit. This goes for both freestanding birth centers and hospital birth centers.

Explain your situation and ask what accommodations they will make for you. Ask if a private room is possible. Ask if you may have a room relatively isolated from mothers with healthy babies. (I joked that they stuck me in the solitary confinement unit, but I never did hear another baby cry. My mother says she did. Maybe angels had their hands over my ears.)

Ask about early release from the hospital, and if they say that's possible, ask how you can get a nurse visit at home to check on your recovery. My nurse played dirty with me and got me to sign my discharge paperwork before saying the hospital had decided not to provide a nurse visit if I checked out early.

Find out if (and how) they will mark your door to alert staff to your loss or impending loss. Apparently they marked the door at my hospital, but I forgot to ask how, and I never saw it on the door to take it home with me.

Request nurses specially trained in bereavement if possible.

Ask about your options for recovery outside the maternity unit. This is not always the best option (a postpartum woman needs to be treated by nurses familiar with postpartum needs) but you may be comforted to know if it's available.

If someone assures you a certain request will be granted, be sure to take his or her name. "Judy Smith authorized rooming-in" will carry more weight in a crisis than "But someone said!"

ORGAN DONATION, ETC.

If you are morally comfortable with organ donation and the like, speak to your doctor ahead of time about what preparations will need to be made. Find out how the donations will be handled and whether that will impact the time you have with your baby.

Some parents find it comforting to think that their baby's body has helped others.

Organ donation is somewhat controversial, so look into the current state of affairs before you make a decision. If the cause of death will be the removal of the organs, that's in the realm of "organ harvesting," and it's morally problematic. In the case of anencephaly, we were told Emily's organs couldn't be donated at all.

Other options that are less morally problematic:
- Tissue donation
- Cord blood donation
- Breast milk donation

If you want to donate breast milk, contact the milk bank ahead of time to find out what hoops you'll need to jump through in order to qualify as a donor. You'll also want to learn what kind of equipment you'll need to collect the milk according to their guidelines.

(The worst nurse in the world refused to listen to me about the required blood test for donating breastmilk. She mocked me, then made a big show of calling the blood lab and providing them all the wrong information, then admitting that yes, her patient was being very unreasonable. A moment later she looked up to discover this postpartum bereaved mother standing over her, face white with rage, shouting that since it was too much trouble for her to do her damn job, I'd go home and open a vein and bleed straight into the test tube. Suddenly she was willing to sign the form. I'm not a very nice person.)

If it's possible to donate cord blood, you'll want that worked out far in advance of the birth because there will be specific collection procedures involved. (My hospital screwed that up too, by the way. The guy in the lab got the clamped cord, and because he'd never done this kind of procedure before, he threw it out. I asked Emily's spirit to go steal his car keys. I'm not a very nice person.)

If you are involved in any kind of study that requires collecting tissue or blood samples, get written instructions in advance and make sure everyone on staff has a copy. Hospital machinery often gets going in such a way that there's little room for anything unusual. (See the lab tech above, who perhaps has just replaced his fifth set of keys.) Pester them just enough that they actually remember to get whatever samples are required by the study.

SIBLINGS

Beyond a certain age, siblings seem to appreciate the time spent with the baby. They may be apprehensive about holding a baby who seems very fragile, though, or that they're afraid will die in their arms. As you'll do with the funeral afterward, ask what the child wants to do at every step of the way, and give your child a way out of the situation (which may mean delegating one relative as the person to take the child for a walk down to the cafeteria). Children will generally know what they can handle.

Some siblings will want to look at the baby; others will not. Some will want to hold the baby; others will be content to sit beside the baby while you hold the baby. Virtually anything is acceptable. If Rule One is to love your baby, it kind of goes without saying that you're also parenting your other child(ren) with love. You know your child, and you're in charge of this part.

My son was not frightened of Emily's appearance or her impending death. Provided with an opportunity to hold her (while seated in my lap) he did. Afterward, when talking about Emily, he said, "I held my sister." And he said it with a smile.

My son was not present at my daughter's actual birth, but some feel that's an important part of bonding. That is a decision to be made within the family itself, and in accordance with your birth attendant's practices.

RELATIVES AND OTHER VISITORS

To a point, you may want them there, and some will arguably have a right to visit. Make sure the hospital will allow them to enter immediately after the birth, no matter what time it is, since your baby may not arrive during visiting hours. You don't want them to miss out on a chance to meet your baby just because the regulations say they ought to show up at 9 a.m.

Some things to consider: how many people you want crowded into a hospital room with you; the length of time you expect them to stay (we allowed the grandparents to stay until after Emily died; in retrospect, we might have considered sending them away so we could have more time alone with her); and how soon after the birth you want them invited in (we waited until Emily and I were cleaned up, which was about as long as it took them to make the drive to the hospital).

Do try to make sure everyone maintains the solemnity of the moment. If Uncle Fred is going to prattle on and on about his car's transmission problems, someone needs to be instructed ahead of time to keep him quiet. Nicely. But still.

RELIGIOUS OBSERVANCES

If you want a religious ceremony to mark the child's life, such as a baptism or a dedication, speak ahead of time to the hospital chaplain and your clergy. Find out what you can do yourself in case time is of the essence. Some opt against any particular rite, feeling that they are "for the living" and therefore their baby will not need it, but if you do want some kind of rite, set it up in advance.

A special note for Catholics: any person (non-Catholics or non-Christians alike) can baptize someone into the Catholic faith using any water. They need to sprinkle or pour water on the baby's forehead while saying, "I baptize you in the name of the Father, and of the Son, and of the Holy Spirit." We actually put this into the birth plan because it was important to us.

In case your baby is stillborn, a baptism can be performed anyhow; in that case, it is called a conditional baptism, and the procedure is the same except for the wording: "If you are able to be baptized, I baptize you in the name of the Father, and of the Son, and of the Holy Spirit." Emily was baptized by my husband using this formula because at birth we weren't sure she was still alive.

I want to stress something here: God is not limited by human ritual. I've spoken to parents whose baby was stillborn, and they often feel a deep grief and confusion that through no fault of theirs, the baby died before birth and was unable to be baptized. Can the baby still go to heaven? Where is their baby now?

Years later, Catholic writer Mark Shea said something on the National Catholic Register blog that caught my eye.

"We are bound to receive grace through the sacraments; God is not bound to only give it through the sacraments. Sacraments are not reducing valves designed to keep the dispensation of grace to a minimum. They are the kisses of

God: the place where He promises us He will always meet us. If He wishes, He can meet us other places as well."

In other words, the sacrament of baptism confers certain graces and privileges to the human soul, but that doesn't mean God's hands are tied if a baby dies before birth. Of course God can still bless your baby as He sees fit. God is limitless. It's a misunderstanding of the sacraments to interpret them as limiting God.

My friend Scott, who had studied for the Catholic priesthood, wrote to me while I was pregnant to let me know that Catholics can request that their baby, in danger of death, could even receive confirmation, and that any priest may confirm in case of danger of death. He said, "The character conferred by confirmation will endure unto eternity and conform your baby more to Christ forever. At any rate it was drummed into me in theology that it was a priest's duty to confirm in such circumstances."

He added, "The relevant canons for confirmation of infants are 883-3; 889 and 891. By canon law baptism, confirmation, and the funeral are a parish priest's responsibility. Canon 530 begins: 'The functions especially entrusted to the parish priest are as follows:

1) the administration of baptism;

2) the administration of the sacrament of confirmation to those in danger of death in accordance with can. 883 n.3;

5) the conduct of funerals.'"

We requested confirmation for Emily, and the hospital chaplain was able to do it.

PHOTOGRAPHS AND VIDEOS

Take photos. Take lots of photos.

I would recommend video too, but it's very hard for me to watch the video, and on the video I noticed some aggravating things I hadn't noticed at the time. (By the way, in the time it took you to read that sentence, someone ought to have taken three pictures.)

Make sure you have at least two cameras working. We had four cameras for Emily's birth, and one of those didn't get any pictures because of a malfunction. (Take another photo—it's been too long.) Ask the nurses to help you take photos, and designate one of your visitors as the photographer after he or she has had a chance to visit with the baby. My brother took over as videographer and did an excellent job. My mother took many, many photos on my camera after hers had problems. (Take another photo.)

Remember, if you take the photos and you hate them, you can always discard them later. But you'll only have one chance to get them.

Note for those as clueless as I was: many hospitals dim the lights for the birth. Remember to turn them up a bit before you start taking photographs. We didn't, and some of the photos are very dark.

A few other tips:
- Make sure to get a lot of face-forward shots. Afterward, you'll want to remember your baby's face most of all.
- Take pictures of the whole baby: hands, feet, whole body. Most of Emily's photos have her wrapped tight

in a blanket and wearing a hat. We were keeping her warm, of course, but after she died I made sure to get those other pictures.
- Black and white photos may be your friend. Babies with discoloration from birth will look very normal in black and white prints. Play with rendering your pictures in black and white or sepia tones. If you can't bear to do it yourself, ask a friend with photo editing software (you know, one of the thousands of people who said, "If there's anything I can do." Yes, here's something you can do. Greyscale these fifty-five pictures.) You can get photo editing software for free or pay a little for Photoshop Elements.
- If your baby has a visible deformity, as with anencephaly, don't shy away from photographing that part. Keeping it covered may be preferable for the shots you show other people, but you will have some parent-only shots too. We took only one picture of Emily's uncovered head, but it was from a distance, and now I don't have a good picture of how plum-shaped her little head was. Again, if you don't like it afterward, you can discard it.
- After your baby dies, do continue to take pictures, but I caution against leaving the baby in the bassinette to take them. Babies belong in someone's arms. They look better snuggled.
- Be prepared for the photos to make your baby seem darker and more beat-up than she looked at the time. See above with photo editing software: you can

probably ask a professional to adjust the colors for you.
- Hey, it's been too long since you took a picture.

Afterward you may well ask, as I did, how can one life be boiled down to a hundred crappy photos? The answer my friend gave was, "It can't," but at least we have that many. If you can get even more, that may be a comfort. Snap away.

NILMDtS

In the years since Emily was born, photographers have begun volunteering as an organization called Now I Lay Me Down to Sleep. These are professionals who will come to the hospital to photograph you and your baby.

While I have no personal experience with these incredibly generous photographers, I've seen their photos. The level of skill and the emotional vulnerability they bring to this job is unmatched. If they have a volunteer in your area, I strongly urge you to make contact with them and ask about their services.

Their website is at nowilaymedowntosleep.org

THINGS TO SAY, SING, AND DO

I found it helpful to "rehearse" the scene ahead of time in my mind to determine what was important to me to say and do with Emily in however long we had with her. Rehearsing helped me remember when the time came. I forgot the things I had wanted to do that I didn't rehearse. I remembered the ones I did (call it self-programming).

Some things are simply natural and will come on cue, like snuggling your baby or rocking your baby. Others have told me they sang lullabies or read books. Rule One: Love your baby. You get to decide how you do that in the hospital, and if possible, I want you to have the fewest regrets about things you forgot in the rush of the moment.

Here's something interesting: days after Emily died, I became very upset that I'd never kissed her. What kind of idiot mother doesn't kiss her own baby? But when we watched the video, evidence shows that I kissed her at least a dozen times.

But if you decide what's important to you ahead of time, it will feel natural when you do it in the moment. For example, it's important to me for some reason for people to feel like they don't need to hang on for the sake of those they're leaving behind. So when the time came, I said to Emily, "It's okay if you have to leave us. It's okay if you have to let go." And she did. It makes me feel marginally better to know she left with my blessing.

Some things are definites: give your baby lots of cuddles and kisses. Touch and talk are always good. If you have special outfits for your baby to wear, bring them and ask for help dressing her. If you want to bathe your baby, make sure you get the chance to do so. If your baby is born alive, encourage her to hold your finger (I don't remember doing that) and even try nursing or feeding colostrum from a spoon. If you want the baby to stay in your room for several hours after the death, demand that right. The baby is your baby, not the hospital's baby, and you have the right to stay with your baby.

HOSPITAL STAFF

And that brings us to another type of potentially clueless individual: the nursing staff. If you've toured the birth center in advance and explained your situation, you may well get bereavement-trained nurses who won't pop in full of joy as they ask with delight, "So, what are you having?" ("A baby. Now leave and return without that fake smile.")

But the rest of the hospital won't know unless your door is marked. (And even then, some people are so into a routine that they won't check for markers.) So you may have to deal with a very cheerful phlebotomist, an orderly who wants to make sure you know how her grandkids slept through the night, and a meal service worker who is bursting with congratulations. Treat them the way you treated clueless strangers: a very numb "Thank you" should suffice.

You're still going to be a conundrum to the employees who do know your situation and who are prepared to deal with bereavement.

Even the most sensitive hospital employee may not know how to handle your situation since you knew in advance that your baby wouldn't survive. And you've pre-grieved. And you're not in shock. Well, not as in shock as if you had to process the information, the questions, and the reality all at the same time. You'll still be in shock, just less shocky.

Several very kind staff members tried to impart to me their philosophy about neonatal death, all of which I took with "Uh-huh" and a bland smile because I'd had five months to work out my philosophy about neonatal death a) at my leisure and b) from the driver's seat. I suggest you listen for the heart behind their words even when their words don't pertain to you at all.

They'll expect you to be hysterical, and if you're not, you may feel abnormal. You're not. You just knew in advance and did some of the hard work up front.

As long as they're there, though, make them take photos. They'll feel better to know they've been helpful.

A BIRTH PLAN TEMPLATE

Here you go, a list of things to put in your birth plan:

An introduction where you thank the staff for looking out for you in a very difficult situation.

Things you want for labor and delivery, such as preferred methods of pain management, what kind of surroundings you would like, whether you want food, who should be allowed in the room, and how you feel about medications.

What you want as regards fetal monitoring, since you may have a choice about that.

Your options for a surgical birth if it comes to that, and episiotomy versus a natural tear.

What you want done right after the birth with regard to assessing and treating your baby.

Who you would like to cut the cord.

A declaration that the baby will stay with you at all times.

Hospital personnel you would like to speak with after the birth, such as a lactation consultant, a chaplain, etc.

EMILY'S BIRTH PLAN

Birth Plan for Emily Rose

Due July 3rd, 2000

Written by Jane (mother) and James (father)

We have written this birth plan for our daughter Emily, who has been diagnosed with anencephaly. We have chosen the midwives of [...] to deliver our daughter at [...] because of their reputation as caring practitioners and their high level of medical expertise. We hope this birth plan is of assistance in guiding the decisions which must be made during the course of our daughter's birth.

We are not closed to ideas outside of this birth plan, but these should serve as a guideline. We believe that the following requests will help us make the most of our limited time with Emily.

Labor and Delivery:

1) Jane would like to freely change position during labor. She requests suggestions regarding positions for laboring and later for birth, in the hopes that a proper position can help to diminish pain and make contractions more effective. If laboring in water is possible, please show Jane how to make best use of it.

2) Should pain medication become necessary, Jane prefers to start with a sedative rather than a narcotic. **NO MORPHINE.** Jane has terrible reactions to morphine. If a narcotic is administered, please consider that Nubain worked well during her last labor. If an epidural, please use an ultra low-dose epidural so Jane can assist with pushing.

Please keep in mind that our main objective is for Jane to remain as alert as possible.

3) Assuming they do not rupture on their own, please do not rupture the amniotic membranes artificially. Other mothers of anencephalics have found the membranes and fluid will help protect the baby's head during labor and delivery. We feel this will increase Emily's chances of being born alive.

4) Jane would like to deliver in a squatting or semi-squatting position if she is able. Please help if she can't figure out the positioning on her own. Please take other measures to

relax/stretch the perineum before resorting to episiotomy. Please allow Jane to push at her own pace.

5) If delivery by cesarean, James is to remain with Jane at all times.

If relatives are waiting or phone in, we request that a nurse please give them updates as applicable.

After the Birth:

6) Because Emily may die immediately before or after birth, James will baptize her immediately. In the event that James is unavailable or unable to baptize her, one of the birth attendants should dip her fingertips in water (any kind) and using that, make the sign of the cross on Emily's forehead while saying the words "I baptize you in the name of the Father, and of the Son, and of the Holy Spirit. Amen." This is very important to us.

7) If the diagnosis of anencephaly is correct, we request only temporary assistance to initiate Emily's breathing. After that, comfort measures only. Emily is not to be placed on artificial life support without permission of either Jane or James. (Note: if the diagnosis was incorrect, take whatever medical measures are necessary, but please keep both parents completely informed.)

8) We request that Emily be immediately handed to her father or mother, depending on the circumstances.

9) James may or may not want to cut the cord. Please ask his preference at the time.

10) Emily is to remain with her parents at all times.

Because we don't know how long Emily will survive, we want to spend time with her immediately after delivery. Please delay any procedures that can be put off until later. With routine and necessary procedures, please perform as many as possible with Emily in her parents' arms. For the rest, James will accompany Emily and return her to Jane as soon as possible.

11) Emily is to receive some kind of nutrition. Our first preference is breast milk. Jane would like to try nursing Emily immediately after birth. If this is not possible, Jane would like to express breast milk. We will bring our own Haberman Feeder, but we are open to suggestions of other feeding methods which may be easier and more effective for our daughter.

12) We would like assistance in taking photographs. We may have a video camera as well. Please help us with that also if we require assistance.

13) If Emily dies during our hospital stay, please notify staff members as applicable. Please allow us space to grieve without abandoning us. We would like time alone to hold Emily after her death to say our goodbyes.

Keepsakes Requested:

- bassinet card
- hats
- baby blanket
- any photographs taken at the hospital
- hospital ID bracelet
- hand and footprints
- molds of both hands and both feet (we have kits with us)
- lock of hair
- we are open to other suggestions as well

Signed:

_____

Jane

_____

James

BLUE MOON BABY

BY Jane Lebak

Blue moon baby
Harvest moon girl
Heart like the flawless wax
of an unburnt candle
Spirit upright as a redwood
straight as a wick never married to flame
Soul a wisp of smoke that escapes
like a breathy sigh rising in the chill
Sleeping eyes blue like the stars that surround
the harvest moon

FUNERAL PLANNING

And now for the part nobody likes to think about. I urge you to make most of these decisions early, though. After your baby's death, you don't want to be having to make dozens of decisions which will be unalterable should you change your mind later. I urge both parents to discuss the issues with one another before venturing out and gathering facts from the professionals. Preparing for your baby's death will not cause your baby to die. Planning does not indicate a lack of faith in God. Miracles are wonderful, but we can't plan on them happening, or else they'd be called commonplaces.

All these plans can be undone in an instant if your baby is miraculously cured. But it will take a while to get them in place, and it's better to handle each issue separately while you're clearheaded and have some sort of energy. The preparations will also put your mind at ease once they're completed.

I know this section is tough. I'll give you two breathers in the middle.

COST

Everyone knows horror stories about how much funerals cost in America. I have no idea what they cost anywhere else in the world, so let that be my caveat. The decisions you make may be affected by money considerations, which is why I lead off with money, prosaic as that might be.

I decided sometime in March that if we were going to be burying a baby in July, and if it was going to cost us thousands of dollars, we needed to know immediately so we could budget for it. Practical, right? What did I learn?

I learned that if I wanted to, I could bury my baby for free. $0.00.

At every step of the way, there was a free option available to me if I wanted or needed to take it. Even if I didn't want that option, the various professionals were "willing to work with the parents." This was in the year 2000, but people didn't just recently invent greed. The professionals in the funeral industry know you've got a special circumstance, and crass as this may sound, you also have time to shop around. If someone treats you badly while you're making arrangements (and yes, someone did) go find someone else to work with (and yes, I did that too). But just based on price, I learned we'd be okay.

Cremation would have been free.

The Catholic cemetery would have given us the grave plot for free if we never put a marker on it.

The plots at the municipal cemetery ranged from $50 to $150 for a baby-size grave on which you could put a small marker. The sizes of the plots ranged from nine square feet (three by three) to a little smaller. There was a cost for opening the grave (some called it a burial cost) and it ranged from $50 to $100. There's also a fee for placing the marker on the site, but I never found out how much that was because the folks who made our stone "forgot" to factor that into the cost.

Caskets for adults generally cost thousands of dollars. For an infant, go down by two orders of magnitude. The average cost for a casket that we saw was $100. The cheapest was $80; the most expensive was $150 (and I have been told that model looked like an Igloo cooler). Trappist Caskets out of Iowa makes free caskets for infants (and they ship all over the U.S.) https://trappistcaskets.com/infant/

We ended up paying $120 because we wanted a slightly larger casket that fit both Emily and her too-large Snuffles bear.

Baby caskets currently on the market are mostly self-vaulting, meaning you don't need to pay extra for a concrete vault at the cemetery.

A word of warning: infant caskets are impossibly tiny. I opted not to take a look early on because the support group moms warned me not to; the funeral directors were willing to let me see one, but they urged no. I'm glad I didn't. The first casket they wanted to use was the size of a jewelry box. If I had seen that before Emily was born, they'd have had to scrape me off the carpet with a spatula. The second size up was about the size of a countertop microwave oven.

Obituaries cost differently from paper to paper. In ours, the obit was free but the death notice cost $45 because it had more information. If you choose to have prayer cards or thank-you notes printed up, they'll run about $20. Birth announcements seem to cost as much as wedding invites, if you can believe it, if you have a professional printer run them off. Emily's announcements cost $75 for 50, but the copy shop guy ran off an extra twenty for us. Nowadays, I'd suggest just going to Vistaprint or Shutterfly to print your own announcements. The online services will let you do most of the design in advance and then you can plug in the information afterward. (Or visit your local copy shop guy. I have no idea why, but the guys who run copy shops just always seem to be the friendliest people in town.)

We had a full funeral for our daughter, although there was a free option available here too if we wanted to just take over one of the daily Masses. The presence of the priest was free, but we paid about $200 to rent the church. (Afterward, we had free use of the church hall to feed our guests.) The gravestone was probably our biggest expense, and it ran about $350, but again, there were both cheaper and more expensive options available. The funeral home could have given us a brass plaque with Emily's name slid into it for practically nothing, or we could have opted against having a marker at all.

Some organizations, such as the Knights of Columbus, offer a death benefit to members who have lost a baby, so if you need help financing any of this, it's worth checking any groups you belong to.

In sum, while you can always spend up to the moon to bury your baby, it would be more reasonable to assume you'll spend anywhere from $750 to nothing at all. So now that you're armed with that info, how do you go about making decisions?

FUNERAL HOME

You'll probably need to work with a funeral home. They'll be able to navigate the paperwork for you, and trust me, when you're dealing with a child's death, you want that paperwork to be in order. (And even so, Emily's death certificate came back with the wrong date on it. Blame the doctor.) The funeral home will also act as your go-between with the cemetery and with the presider at the memorial service (should you want one). It's also good to have someone around to tell you what to do and where to sit and what's happening next.

How to choose? I didn't have the option of asking friends who had buried their family members. Lucky me, I was the first in my circle. When I asked at our church, I was given the names of all the local ones, in no particular order. In case you're wondering, this was unhelpful.

I chose a small funeral home that was listed in our bulletin. They were extremely nice to me, and I got the sense that they were being up front whenever they explained something. I was only seven months pregnant at the time, so maybe they had more incentive to be nice.

They put everything in writing (I think this was required by federal law) and they even showed me the receipt for the baby casket they would use. I would be charged no more than they had been charged. The home was a family-run operation, and I dealt with the son.

The father joined us halfway through, and as the son was running off some photocopies, the father talked very bluntly with me about various options. He looked sad and was very straightforward. He also said, "I don't make any money off babies." I get the impression that not every funeral home is like that, though. I would advise starting early and not letting anyone bully you. Most areas have more than one funeral home, and if not, a neighboring town probably does.

Ask them what services they'll charge you for. Ask if they will transport your baby's body from the hospital to the funeral home and from the funeral home to the cemetery (or to the site of the funeral); if you want to transport your baby from the hospital yourself, ask how they accommodate that.

Ask what their role will be during the funeral or memorial service. Ask if they have a "cold room" for storing your baby's body so the mother has time to recover between birth and the burial.

Make sure you have the option of dressing your baby yourself and watching the casket get sealed so you know everything you put in stays there.

If you want embalming, find out how long that will take. Ask if the casket is self-vaulting. If you want to personalize the casket ahead of time, like with your other kids' handprints or stickers or other artwork, ask if you can bring it home and how far ahead of the birth you should bring it back.

Ask about options if you want to transport the casket from this cemetery to a different cemetery in the future. (I was told one model was better for that than the other.) Ask about options for a viewing at the funeral home if that's what you want.

FUNNY STORY

You'd think in this business they'd have to be nice, but my mother tells this story about a funeral director in Brooklyn, New York.

When my great aunt died, my mother needed to phone my brother long distance from the funeral parlor to tell him when the funeral was. The pay phone ate my mother's change, so she tracked down the funeral director, a creepy woman, to ask if she could use the office phone.

The woman snapped, "Well, make it quick!"

My mother was fuming, but she dialed my brother while the woman glared at her. And then, of course, she got a busy signal.

The woman was still glaring.

My mother's hand tightened on the phone. How dare that woman? Seriously, the family was spending thousands on a funeral, and the director was treating her like a criminal for using the phone when it was the funeral home's pay phone that hadn't worked in the first place?

So my mom shouted into the receiver, "Your mother's dead!" and slammed the phone back onto the hook.

Then she turned to the funeral director, who looked stunned. Mom smiled sweetly. "Was that quick enough?"

EMBALMING

You do not have to embalm your baby.

If you choose not to embalm your baby, you may not be allowed to have an open-casket service. Check your state laws. However, there is no legal mandate that every person be embalmed, and some religions even forbid it.

Some funeral directors want the money, though, and will tell you babies over a certain weight need to be embalmed. Ask to see the book on that, and while they're scrambling to regain composure, find another funeral home.

(A friend of mine suggests saying, sincerely, "Go and find that statute online and print it out for me on that printer over there. I'll wait." I've found that's useful in any number of situations where someone tells me it's the law to do X, Y, or Z, and I know darned well it's not.)

CEMETERIES

Most cemeteries put all the babies in the same place because they have smaller graves.

Visit the baby yard. Find out if you are able to have a gravestone and if so, if it can be an upright marker and what size they permit. (Find out for me about that one odd-size marker that every cemetery always seems to have! For Pete's sake, why do some people get 24" x 24" markers while every other baby can only have 8" x 16"?)

Ask if you're allowed to lay down cut flowers. Ask if you can plant flowers. Ask if you can leave toys, lawn ornaments, or other decorations. Find out if they are open year-round and if they allow burials year-round. (Maybe it's an urban legend, but I've heard that in some places they limit burials to non-winter months because otherwise they'd have to dynamite open the frozen ground).

Ask what their daily visiting hours are and what days they're open.

Listen for traffic noises. But don't let that be your deciding factor. Emily's grave is about 40 feet from one of the busiest roads in the city and I never heard the traffic when I visited her, no matter how long I stayed

You may want to visit frequently afterward, so keep that in mind while making decisions. I initially didn't want the cemetery we chose because I would pass it nearly every day. Later I found its central location was a comfort, though, because even when I couldn't stop in, I could still glance as I drive past and make sure things looked okay. I find it funny that when someone else is in that part of the cemetery, I feel protective of my daughter.

LET'S TAKE ANOTHER BREAK FROM THE HEAVY STUFF FOR A MOMENT

When we pulled up to the funeral home to interview them, I parked right in front of their big sign.

My son looked up at it and grinned. "F-U-N. That spells fun!"

I didn't have the heart to tell him no.

He also loved when we went to the monument makers. "Momma, this is a cemetery store!"

Okay, break's over.

CREMATION VERSUS BURIAL

This is a personal decision, to be made in accord with your beliefs and your preferences.

(Note for Catholics: Catholics may be cremated, allowed by changes in Church guidelines in the '70s, I believe. The ashes must be laid in a permanent grave in an individual container, though, not scattered or mixed with others' ashes.)

Personally, I like having a safe place to go just to think about Emily. I imagine that if she were in an urn on my mantle, she'd get lost in the clutter. I know others are comforted by keeping the ashes in the home.

Cremation may cost less, so ask about this at the funeral home.

TRANSPORT

Someone has to take your baby's body to the cemetery or the funeral home. In many states, you can apply for a permit to do this yourself. I know some mothers and fathers have special memories of that one last trip.

We would have been the first in our state to apply for this permit, so we didn't do it.

When the funeral home transported Emily to the church, they used a silver minivan, and it looked very nice, for what it's worth. Using my car with cartoon stickers all over the outside and a cartoon-themed vanity plate would have been...well not exactly somber, to say the least.

(We didn't have pallbearers. Her casket was small enough that the funeral director walked with it to the front of the church looking very stately, and set it on a stand. At the end of the funeral, he brought it back to the minivan.)

SONGS

If you have songs you want to use at the funeral, talk to the presider ahead of time, and talk to the musicians too.

Our church musician grandly blew us off, and by 9:30 the night before the funeral still hadn't talked to us about which songs we wanted. So much for rehearsal time. We think she wanted to waltz in at the last minute and do just the songs she always did for everyone else's funeral. You know, it's been over a decade, I still think of that woman with irritation. That was my daughter. How *dare* she?

Instead, a very good friend from our old church's choir played, played my guitar, and she did a beautiful job. She played all the songs we wanted instead of forcing us to use her own repertoire, which The Disappearing Vocalist was being stubborn about.

When our friend played the refrain from Weston Priory's "I Have Loved You" as the casket was incensed, everyone around us wept. So my suggestion her? Pick songs you love. Make contact with the musician early on, and if the church's preferred musician acts like a prima donna, fire her. You'll be happier that way.

THE INFAMOUS BLACK DRESS (APPLICABLE TO MOTHERS ONLY)

This is the detail I've always used to describe what my website was about: "How to pick out a funeral dress for postpartum when you're eight months pregnant." You say that and people suddenly "get" the enormity of what you're doing.

You need to decide now what you're going to wear to the funeral. Your normal wardrobe might not fit you three days after childbirth; your maternity wardrobe might not fit you then either. Like everything else, you'll find yourself stuck in a twilight time.

To make the conundrum marginally better, what you wear doesn't have to be a black dress. I know of many mothers who wore pink or yellow to their baby's funeral. I wanted black, however, and I owned no summertime black dresses. I was also eight months pregnant when I finally faced the reality that this problem was not going to solve itself.

There are two major dilemmas here. First, a postpartum woman's abdomen will still be a bit flabby after giving birth. I've heard from women who couldn't fit into their pre-pregnancy clothes months afterward; but some women (ta-dah) are back in loose clothes in a matter of days.

Second, and much more important, if you have the burial relatively soon after giving birth, your breasts will be massively engorged. Massively. I looked like I'd had 25 implants. Thankfully the engorgement goes away quickly, but you need to know you'll be top-heavy and possibly leaking while wearing the dress. And sensitive, too. Ouch.

Some women wear a maternity dress. This seems like a good idea, though I didn't do it. Maternity dresses are frequently designed in layers and are expandable and contractable without too much hassle.

If you think you'll want your maternity clothes burned immediately afterward (I packed mine away the first instant I could zip my largest pair of shorts!) look for a dress a size up from your pre-pregnant size, maybe with a jacket, maybe something you can cinch up or leave loose, so there's some "play" in the garment.

Leave room for LOTS of breast expansion. You may want to make sure the neckline is fairly high if you are going to be wearing a sports bra after birth. A loose black blazer might be good to keep on hand as well.

Side note: buy disposable nursing pads to put in your bra. You'll be crying during the funeral; you don't need to be leaking milk in addition to that. (Although a loose blazer will help with covering that as well.)

THINGS TO PUT IN THE CASKET

We put into Emily's casket a teddy bear with a big friendly face, a Mizpah coin, and a letter I wrote to her on the spur of the moment before we went to get her dressed.

Right before we closed the casket, I snipped off a bit of my hair and put it in with her.

Emily is wearing a red onesie with lace trim and a white lace bonnet, and she's wrapped in a soft white blanket. On the onesie, we pinned a tiny gold cross and a guardian angel/miraculous medal pin a good friend gave me after the diagnosis. (I thought that was especially sweet since the gift-giver is Jewish.)

If you're not familiar with a Mizpah coin, it's a pair of necklaces with a coin that's been split into two pieces. It says, "May the Lord watch between me and thee while we are apart from one another." I've seen other means of doing the same thing: hearts split in half or nested hearts. I wanted one in three pieces (one for each parent and one to be buried with her) but couldn't find it, even on websites specifically selling these necklaces for babies who had died. Am I the only one who thought the father would also like a keepsake? We buried one half with her, and the other half is in her memory box.

Other people have told me they put similar things into the casket. Some asked the baby's siblings to contribute items; others asked the grandparents. What you put into the casket is up to you, but consider having duplicate items so you can keep one for yourself. Also consider that some items associated with your baby may be too precious to you, so it's okay to change your mind.

One thing to keep in mind is that there won't be very much room in the casket, so pack small.

MEMENTOS AT THE FUNERAL

If you're really organized, you might be able to put together a program for the funeral. Sadly, I wasn't, so everyone kind of muddled through our service following our cues. (Again, see your friendly neighborhood copy shop guy!)

We set up a little display at the church entrance with a tiny photograph album that had my father's pictures of Emily in it, plus a trimmed-down photo of Emily and my son in a frame a friend gave us. And a basket with a memorial gift for anyone who attended. (A memento? I'm not sure what other people call it.)

We had a guest book, and I'd heartily recommend one because there were people there I didn't even realize had come! (You can make sure guests put in their addresses by having a friend sign first and put all the right info. The guests at my brother's wedding all just put their names.

That's a nightmare when you need to write thank-you notes.)

We had the funeral home print up prayer cards for us with Emily's name and dates. For the back of the card, they had twenty-eight poems and prayers you could choose from. They provided a similar choice of images for the front of the card, so that was pretty easy.

We also offered packets containing wildflower seeds to be planted in Emily's memory. We used a place called Tree Beginnings that has since turned into Plant a Memory. The seed packets were usually sold for weddings, so it was a real thrill to visit their website and find that every single type of packet said, "Thank you for attending the start of our new life together." One phone call later, we clarified that it was possible to have a blank seed packet.

(When the Tree Beginnings rep found out why I was ordering them blank, she was very cordial and put a no-charge rush on them. She told me they'd be ready in two weeks; I had them in five days. So remember whenever you're struggling with the Clueless that there are a lot of Clueful people out there too, and when some of them have leverage to be nice to you, they'll quietly do so.)

Here's a learn-from-my-failure tip: if you put out the prayer cards and seed packets, or anything else for your funeral attendees, state clearly that everybody is to take *one*. You know, one person, one thingie. This is common sense, right? No, it's not. I suspect people were filling their pockets with Emily's seeds, because we had about 35 guests for the funeral (many of them couples) and more than sixty seed packets, but *poof.* If you noticed any forests sprouting in your area about two decades ago, let me know. I'll start a petition to call it the Emily Rose Memorial Forest.

One family gave me a letter to share on the website in honor of their daughter Brianna. They handed out this letter at the funeral to explain more about Brianna's condition, why it happens, and how they felt about the privilege of carrying their little girl for as long as they could. In their letter they also shared suggestions about organizations for making memorial donations. I think this is a terrific idea, so I'm passing it along for your consideration.

BUT WHAT IF...

Through all these plans, it lurks at the back of your mind.

WHAT IF THE DIAGNOSIS WAS WRONG OR A MIRACLE OCCURS?

Let's say you have your baby and everything is perfect. Wow.

I didn't go through this, but I've heard third-hand or fourth-hand of families who have. I've also been on the sidelines of a pregnancy with a woman whose baby was being constantly diagnosed with lethal issues and then, on repeat ultrasounds, the previously diagnosed issues would be said to have "resolved" and the radiologist would diagnose a completely different condition. After a while, my friend thought it began to feel like a witch hunt. At birth, the baby was fine.

You probably think to yourself, Oh Happy Dilemma! If the doctors and radiologists are all wrong, the worst possible thing that will happen is that you have to go home and throw together a nursery. You might have to co-sleep for a few days until your friend can drag a crib out of her attic, and the baby might end up outfitted entirely from the hospital gift shop.

If that happens, everyone will be delighted for you, and congratulations.

Keep a few things in mind as you snuggle your little one.

- Talk to a therapist anyhow. You may be reeling from PTSD from having endured five months or longer of the strain of waiting for a death that now will not happen. Get those feelings out.
- Be prepared to feel overprotective. Come up with a strategy to evaluate actual risks to your child versus the exaggerated risks your heart is going to warn you about.
- Come up with a script for telling everyone who has previously been helping you through the pregnancy. Make sure they understand that a misdiagnosis and a miracle are both extraordinarily rare things, so they shouldn't blow off the next woman who's going through it.
- You may feel "survivor guilt" with the others in your support groups. You'll wonder why your baby survived when theirs didn't. You may even feel ashamed, as though some other mother deserved her baby more than you did. This is something else to discuss with a therapist, or at the very least a supportive friend.

- If anyone from your support group actually accuses you of not deserving your baby as much as someone else did, that person is wrong. People don't get healthy babies just because they deserve them. It's not like babies are handed out as a reward to the virtuous.
- New parents who complain about exhaustion or frustration are sometimes shut up by people saying, "At least you have a healthy baby. That's all that matters." I imagine that would be doubled in case of a true miracle. You are not, however, merely the packaging in which a healthy baby came. Give yourself permission to feel tired when you're tired and frustrated when you're frustrated. Honesty is an awesome thing. If anyone tries to shut you up by saying your baby's health is all that matters, well, they're wrong. You matter too.
- Rule One is to love your baby. Keep abiding by Rule One. And give your little one a kiss on my behalf. Say it's from Emily Rose.

WHAT IF THE BABY LIVES FOR A WHILE?

This is more likely than a miracle, but you might find yourself feeling a lot of the same things. Your baby might be born with his or her birth defect but be in a lot better shape than the doctors predicted. Every so often, someone on one of the support forums would have a baby who lived for two months...or a year.

Especially if the doctors insisted on the absolute worst-case scenarios, you might be in the position of taking home a baby you thought wouldn't live for more than a few minutes, if indeed would be born alive at all. At that point, the doctors may all be standing around unable to help very much (because they are as surprised as you are) and suddenly you're back in uncharted emotional seas.

My suggestions?

While you're still in the hospital, make a list with your pediatrician about exactly what will be required for care at home. Write it out. Get every detail you can imagine. If there are to be bandage changes, medications, round-the-clock feedings, get them on a schedule. If you need special equipment (such as a special feeding tube), write that down and also have the pediatrician make arrangements for you to have a full set before you leave.

My experience with hospitals leads me to believe that once you sign the discharge paperwork, a lot of their concern evaporates, so get everything in place before you sign discharge forms. If some particular care item can be prescribed, get a prescription for it and see if the hospital will fill it for you before you go. If something can only be acquired outside the hospital, send someone to acquire it before you sign out

The hospital may want to discharge you and keep your baby in NICU. Ask if that's really necessary or just for their legal protection. If there's no care they are going to provide in the hospital that you yourself can't provide at home, then provide it at home.

Keep in mind that insurance companies do not deny insurance payment if you leave AMA (against medical advice). A lot of doctors and nurses believe this and will tell you that you will be responsible for your entire hospital bill if you leave without being officially discharged, but that's an urban legend. Look it up online if you aren't sure, or call your particular insurance company.

You probably came to the hospital without a car seat, but many hospitals will loan you a car seat to take the baby home if you don't have one. Ask for them to provide one for you. If the maternity unit doesn't have one, the NICU may have one instead.

Your pediatrician will assure you that you can call 24/7 for advice, and that's the time to get an iron-clad list of reasons you should call the doctor, and then ask the doctor for a direct number. Promise on your heart that you won't call for ridiculous reasons, but for that list you were just given, you don't want to have to call a paging service and try to explain that yes, you know what a seizure looks like and yes, you need them to awaken the doctor. (I've gotten doctors to give me their home numbers. I've never abused that privilege. And keep in mind that if they give it to you, it's a privilege.)

You'll want to come up with a script for talking to medical professionals. Make it along the lines of, "My baby, Emily Rose, was born on July 19th and is diagnosed with anencephaly. She's showing the following symptoms right now." Practice it so that in a moment of crisis, you can be as clear as possible to the people who are prone to patting worried postpartum moms on the head with, "Is this your first baby, dear?" Start with the baby's birthdate and the baby's condition, then the symptom you're calling about, and then, "Doctor Smith-Jones told me to call if we noticed this happening."

A lot of people do labor under the impression that all babies are perfectly healthy and moms manufacture symptoms for their own amusement, so you need to cut through it first. Age. Diagnosis. Symptoms. Request to page the doctor.

Okay, so that's the medical stuff.

My friend told me, "I know you, and if she lives for days, you're not going to sleep at all." I said, "Oh no," but of course she's absolutely right. I wouldn't have slept for days. I've heard from other mothers that they were afraid they'd fall asleep and the baby would have died before they woke up.

Actually, if you don't sleep for five days, *you* will die (that's medically documented) so staying awake on a nigh-eternal basis isn't going to work for either you or your baby.

My suggestion would be to co-sleep if it's possible, that way your baby is right next to you. That might require you to rearrange your furniture a bit or buy the kind of rail you'd use on a toddler bed, but at least you and your baby will be together during the night. If you're worried about rolling over on the baby, my suggestion is to scoot down the bed so your face is parallel to the baby's chest. Follow normal co-sleeping guidelines: if you are on medications that would prevent you from waking up, don't co-sleep. If you have a condition that keeps you from waking up easily, don't do it.

Keep fluffy pillows away from the baby's face. Find the current guidelines for co-sleeping and follow them.

But it's very comforting to be able to awaken during the night and just put your hand onto your baby's chest. And from the baby's perspective, it's physiologically easier on the baby to be near her mother's body and hear her mother's breathing. Your sleep cycles should synchronize, and both of you should in theory sleep better.

If you can't co-sleep or prefer not to, you might be able to get hold of a side-car crib or even just lash a regular crib to the side of the bed with one side removed. This helps the baby stay in a safe sleeping environment and keeps her within reach of your arm. Again, check current guidelines on what's acceptable.

Your emotions will be all over the place. Mom will have postpartum hormones to contend with (which aren't a party even after a healthy birth) and both mom and dad may be dealing with PTSD and survivor guilt *plus* the constant stress of wondering if every day is the last *plus* the physical and emotional demands of caring for a medically fragile baby. Combine that with well-meaning individuals who will be telling you you're lucky to have this much time with your baby, and you may have no idea what to feel.

It will be the same emotions of the pregnancy all over again. Joy: he's with us right now. Dread: he won't be with us forever.

Remember Rule One: love your baby. At the same time, try to take care of yourself.

I would suggest investing in some kind of baby-wearing device, specifically a ring sling. If you find a ring sling awkward, ask around until someone comfortable with it will show you how to use it best. (A La Leche League leader will probably have four such individuals on speed dial. Also check out Babywearing International.) I did buy a ring sling for Emily but never got a chance to use it with her. I used it with subsequent babies and wore it out. There were literally holes in the thing, and I still have it hanging in my closet in case I ever need to carry a baby again.

I recommend a ring sling for two reasons. First, the sling will be more adjustable than a harness and can keep the baby right up against your heart and your hands free while you're walking around. Second, because it's adjustable, you may be able to tuck any medical equipment into the sling and carry that too. A newborn and a tiny oxygen tank will fit easily into a sling.

There are two more reasons a ring sling is a spectacular investment. Consider that the tail of a ring sling is wide and long, and you can cover your baby completely with it if you don't want strangers looking in, trying to touch, or gawking at your baby. And also, consider that to your baby, a sling can feel like a womb outside your body, and having him in a sling will help him feel the movements he became accustomed to while still in utero. He will find this calming and familiar, and the low stress levels will benefit him.

Do not cook while using a baby-wearing device of any sort, and do not drive while wearing one.

Since you have a script for medical staff, have another one for strangers, and just click into it, especially if your baby's birth defect is visible or the baby requires special medical equipment while out in public. Come up with how much information you feel comfortable disclosing, and practice saying that sentence into a mirror until it's reflexive and flat enough to discourage further talk from people you don't need to be talking to.

Also practice a couple of frostily polite shut-them-down remarks for people who are nosy enough to keep demanding information. "My, for a stranger, you certainly are curious," for example. (That's much better than, "If you touch my baby, I'll break your arm in three places and tell the police it was self-defense," which I do not recommend.)

The other parents from your support group will doubtless feel both envy and delight at the same time, so try to keep them updated (for the delight part) but also realize that the still-pregnant mothers are hoping to be just like you while the other mothers are thinking, "Do you know what I could have done with two months?" Please be patient with them, but be aware of their conflicted feelings. Do ask for support when you need it. Don't make every contact with the group about how amazing it is that your baby hit some milestone or another. As with everything, you're going to have to use your best judgment. Remember that these same people will be around for you still, later on, if or when the worst does happen.

Your family members may not be sure what to do either after the first few days, especially if they came to town expecting to attend a funeral a few days after the birth. Don't feel guilty that they traveled, please. (If you have relatives who try to make you feel guilty about not having a funeral yet...that requires a different book. Look for something with "How to deal with narcissists" in the title.) They'll be overjoyed that the baby is still with you, but they'll be unsure that they can actually leave. Because what if...? But they can't stay with you indefinitely, especially if they traveled.

I know: O Happy Dilemma. You'll find yourself solving a lot of problems with that phrase if your baby lives for a few months: O Happy Dilemma, he outgrew the outfits we bought him. O Happy Dilemma, we actually have to make another appointment with the pediatrician. O Happy Dilemma, we need to make decisions about immunizations.

As during the pregnancy, do try to focus on the moments you have now. Be aware that they are an amazing gift, and at the same time don't feel guilty if you don't enjoy every moment of exhaustion or tension. You're human. But since you have the gift of time, treasure that gift. And give your baby a kiss from me.

COPING AFTERWARD AND MEMORIAL IDEAS

Once Emily had died, my father-in-law said to my husband, "You've just done the hardest thing you'll ever do." My husband replied, "I think it's only just starting."

THE HOSPITAL

Personally, I couldn't get out of the hospital fast enough. I delivered Emily a little after 11 p.m. on Wednesday, and I signed out a little after one in the afternoon on Thursday.

The hospital acted very understanding and assured me that because I was leaving so early, I was entitled to one free nurse visit at home to make sure I wasn't bleeding to death. After I signed the discharge papers, the nurse returned and said, "By the way, you can't have a nurse visit."

I'm not the only one who's experienced this switch by hospital staff, so I recommend getting any extras in writing before signing yourself out of the hospital. It stinks to have to be your own advocate hours after your baby's death, but the world is full of predatory and stupid individuals.

SLEEP

The real reason I wanted to leave the hospital was that in a hospital, everyone expects you to be in bed, so visitors march into your room, plop down in a chair, and start entertaining you.

It didn't matter if I was eating lunch, if I had the lights off, if I was under the blankets with my eyes closed. They'd come in and start chatting.

I didn't feel like entertaining or being entertained. I wanted to cry, and I badly needed a nap. At home, if I was in bed with the lights out, visitors interpreted that as, "She's asleep." They stayed in the kitchen and entertained each other.

It's difficult to sleep in those early days after a loss, but do try. I've been told that Tylenol PM is the best sleep medication after a death. It's not a narcotic, just an over-the-counter, and frequently a half-dose will relax you just enough to get to sleep. Ask your care provider if this would be appropriate for you in your circumstances after the death.

(I am not a doctor; my recommendation doesn't count, so don't say I told you to take it. I only said to ask a medical professional if you should take it.)

FLASHBACKS

I relived the birth a number of times, usually at night while not sleeping. Sometimes I'd find myself starting to push at the right point in the scenario, or sitting up in bed and turning around when the nurse would have entered the room. This was scary at first, but after a couple of weeks, the flashbacks faded.

If you're still experiencing flashbacks at your postpartum visit, mention them. If the flashbacks leave you scared, unnerved, or unable to function, ask someone to get you to a therapist right away because you don't have to live that way.

MILK

Your milk will probably come in if you've gone into the third trimester.

Every professional you ask may act surprised, if not stunned, that the stress hasn't suppressed your milk production. Don't believe it. I'm not sure I've ever heard from a mother whose milk production was entirely suppressed by the stress of losing her baby.

I got engorged with about two gallons of milk, to the unbridled delight of my nursing toddler who'd persevered through the last six dry months of the pregnancy. (He looked up after his customary ten-second nurse on the second morning after the birth, got a confused and delighted expression, and said, "Momma, good milk again," then tucked back in and wouldn't even breathe for about fifteen minutes.)

I donated Emily's milk. I pumped out as much as I could, on a schedule, and stuck it into my freezer. Banked milk is vital to the survival of some desperately premature babies, some of whose mothers are unable to produce milk for medical reasons. The early milk, from the first three to five days after the birth, is especially valuable.

While banking Emily's milk didn't "make sense" of her death, it felt like a good thing to do. At least it went into a needy baby's tummy rather than just soaking all my shirts and sheets.

NOT BEING POSTPARTUM

You may have a tendency to act as if you aren't postpartum. After all, a mother who has just given birth should have a baby in her arms. With no baby in yours, you may completely forget that you should be resting, not lifting objects heavier than ten pounds, etc.

Three weeks after the delivery, I found myself exhausted. "What have I done today?" I wondered, and then outlined an entire day where I'd barely sat down going from place to place. Normal for a healthy woman, too much too soon postpartum.

If I'd had a baby, no one would have expected me to do all those things. Without a baby in arms, I felt obliged to get up and run errands as if nothing had happened.

Remind yourself on days you plan too much: your body just delivered a baby. Your blood supply took a hit, your iron reserves are depleted, and it takes six weeks for soft tissue damage to heal. Force yourself to rest.

POSTPARTUM DEPRESSION

Unfair as this is, you may experience postpartum depression in addition to grieving.

The hormonal situation in your body is in wild flux. Your body is making milk, but it's not nursing a baby, and you're starting to make estrogen again, and progesterone levels are crashing, and your thyroid has thrown up its hands in frustration, and your iron levels have plummeted, and…well, it's chaos. Our brains don't do well on a diet of chemical chaos.

And to add to the chemical soup, depression is also a *normal* part of grief. So even without being postpartum, you'd be depressed right now. The question is, how much is too much?

There's no good meter for this. I wish there were.

If you feel you are having undue problems with depression, it will be up to you to determine whether the depression is a part of the grief and needs to be worked through, or whether the depression is hindering the grief and needs to be medicated. And then, once you've figured that out, you'll have to convince your doctor.

(Try to have a sense of humor about this. Teasing apart cause and effect here is like playing the world's largest game of pick-up sticks.)

I'd recommend taking it easy on yourself. The tricks you've used in the past to combat depression may help at this time. I didn't experience postpartum depression after Emily's death even though I had after my son's birth. After Emily's death, I went with my instincts: if I felt like visiting the cemetery, I did. If I felt like crying, I did. If I felt like hiding, I did. If I felt like running away, I ran errands. Most of the early months are blurred, but I think it helped because I never fought my own natural inclinations.

One recommendation is for you to take a list of typical depressive symptoms and rate yourself for every one of them on a scale of one to ten. (You can find depression screenings all over the internet.) Then put that list away and wait a week. At the end of a week, fill it out again. After the next week, fill out a third, and then look at all three of them. Are you showing some improvement? Is it getting worse? If things are getting worse, that's an indicator that you might be stuck and needing help.

Don't downplay your depression. This is hard enough without PPD.

FEELING PREGNANT

This is truly weird, but other mothers said they experienced the same thing I did: pregnancy symptoms even three months after the baby's birth and death.

I found I had an aversion to coffee and alcohol, and nausea after breakfast, but only prior to ovulation (the first 17 days or so of my cycle). Another woman told me that during her pregnancy, hamburgers had triggered her morning sickness, and over a year later, she still couldn't look at a hamburger without feeling queasy.

And then one day, you're sitting there watching television, and you feel the baby kick. The baby you delivered three months earlier.

Phantom kicks are the strangest, most wonderful little haunting you can imagine. I have no idea what causes them, although people like to talk about muscle contractions, gas, the return of abdominal tone…I have no idea. I felt them a couple of times. Lots of women do.

The symptoms and the kicks were disconcerting, and I remember asking if my body itself wasn't longing for my baby. Maybe our bodies themselves can grieve. Maybe in some ways, our bodies remember.

RETURN OF FERTILITY

Even if you are pumping, you should expect your fertility to return quickly. I ovulated at seventeen days postpartum. (When I asked if that was possible, the reply I got was, "It would be a statistical rarity." I replied, should I then take risks and name the resulting child Statistical Rarity Lebak?)

If you're using Natural Family Planning, get in touch with an instructor in your method and review the most current postpartum charting guidelines. The CCL sympto-thermal guidelines as of 2017 were to start charting mucus and temperature as soon as lochia lessens. Once mucus is observed, assume Phase II until ovulation. When I had Emily, the guidelines were substantially different, so again: contact an instructor and get the most current rules.

Pumping milk will not delay your periods the way nursing might. Assume there will be no delay.

My first period postpartum felt like a slap in the face. I was stunned by how all the grief returned with the force of a body blow the moment I saw blood there. It felt wrong. It felt like my body had forgotten her, and it felt like a betrayal. It was like she'd died all over again, and I don't know that there's any way to prepare for that. But if you do feel that way, at least you know you're not alone.

MARCH OF DIMES

The March of Dimes offers a bereavement package to anyone whose baby has died. The kit contains a brief book about dealing with loss, a memory package, and if you give information about your child's cause of death, they can send you a fact sheet. You'll probably know more than the fact sheet, but it's worth taking a look. They may also send you pre-conception guidelines that supposedly maximize your chances of having a healthy baby. Call 1-888-MO-DIMES or visit http://www.marchofdimes.org/bereavement-kit-form.aspx

PHYSICAL EXAM

In addition to your postpartum checkups (which should be at two weeks and six weeks after the loss of a baby) most perinatal loss experts recommend a complete physical four months after the death. They say this because the stress of losing your child may compromise your immune system, and opportunistic infections or other previously undetected problems may begin to go uncontrolled. If your health insurance will let you do this, it seems like a good idea.

CREATIVITY? WHAT'S THAT?

I'M a writer. I was in the middle of a novel when we got the diagnosis, and my writing just...stopped.

And stayed stopped.

And stayed stopped some more.

I put together Emily's website. But fiction? No fiction. I wrote a few poems, but those were short. I said to my friend, "All the humor is gone. All the silly things I used to do. There's nothing there."

Expect your creativity to take a massive hit. If you're an artist or a writer, you may find the art just isn't there. If your work is at least partly in the "pure craft" realm, you may at least be able to go through the motions. If your creativity is mostly in the special touches you put on the everyday work you do...again, you may find it's all mechanical.

This is the Superman story all over again. The parts of your brain that create are now engaged in resolving your grief. Some people create in order to resolve their grief, but for most of us, it's about to stop cold for a while.

This is what I wrote to a friend dismayed by feeling no urge to write whatsoever:

You can "scab over" the hurt, but it's still there, and the trauma hasn't been resolved enough that your inner self—the introspective part that writes—wants to handle it. You may at some level understand that it hasn't been resolved and that's what's keeping you from writing about it. Because it hasn't been resolved, you can't create a tidy little package about it.

For two years, I couldn't write fiction at all. It wasn't until four years later that I actually felt like a writer again. I couldn't explore infant death in fiction until 2005 ("Damage"), but "Damage" centered on the same situation without any grief. It was like the frame of a house without the furnishing, the carpet, or the drapes. I didn't explore the *emotional* connection to infant death until I wrote "Winter Branches" in 2006.

Be patient with yourself. The creativity will come back. Try to nudge it into motion, but if it won't go, then give yourself permission to work on other things and create in other areas. Your energies are occupied in something very important right now.

WHEN TO CREATE IT?

After a tragedy, I would categorize four stages of creativity. The creator:

- is able to record the details of the event; emotion may or may not be present

- creates for catharsis; an emotion-dump, primarily for himself or herself, and the details may or may not be present
- creates evangelistically because there's a Message. E.g., "These were the stupid things people said when Emily died, so you the reader should not say them." (Note that this is outwardly directed, but because it's angry writing, it's still primarily for oneself)
- creates and lets the artwork tell itself without pushing a Message

By Stage 4, the tragedy stops being an Issue, and the artist stops having a Message.

In Stage 2, I don't believe the artist has a Message yet, but s/he's coming toward one. Stage 3 is often unreadable because the Message (and many times an angry Message) dominates the art. The artist is into consciousness-raising and the story takes a back seat to the Message. Unfortunately this phase is where the artist feels fired up and finally ready to write again, and therefore you get most of the writing about Issues, and hence why most issue-exploring writing has a Message.

We process tragedy using many of the same parts of the brain that create artwork. Writing in an effort to process the emotions is journaling, and that's fine. But writing (or painting or sculpting) your tragedy in an attempt to leap right to the end product—that only leads to stalled-out creativity and a burnt-out artist, or else it leads to a fake-sounding resolution.

If you want the processed, final product, those precious resolved feelings, you need to resolve them first.

We create after a tragedy for many reasons, but there's a difference between creating to help yourself and creating to help others. Creating to help others in the same situation requires your feelings to have matured, so take a deep breath. As they say on an airplane, put on your own oxygen mask first.

WHEN THE PIZZA GUY KNOWS YOUR PHONE NUMBER BY HEART

One night as we sat down to dinner, the doorbell rang, and we found the pizza guy, holding a thermal pizza bag. We opened the door and looked at him, and he looked at us. He looked at his receipt and exclaimed, "Oh! It's the same house number, but this isn't the right street." And he added, "If the house number was 25, I figured it had to be you."

Thanks. Thanks so much.

All that is to say, make sure you tip the delivery guy really well because in the postpartum period, after your friends' casseroles are a memory, you may find the lack of creativity extends to a lack of feeling like you want to cook dinner.

THE CEMETERY: TO GO OR NOT TO GO?

One of the nurses who ran the infant loss group said, "When it comes to the cemetery, there are 'goers,' and there are 'not-goers.' And both are fine."

Don't let anyone make you feel guilty about how often you go to the cemetery and how often you do not go to the cemetery. There isn't a scorecard where you punch off holes and after a hundred of them, you get your Excellent Parent Award. No one else gets to tell you how often you should or should not go to the cemetery because no one else feels the comfort or the agitation you experience when you go there.

Does it comfort you? Do it.

Does it agitate you? Don't do it.

Easy-peasy. Rule One is to love your baby. It says nothing about where you have to be to do that.

TOMORROW AND TOMORROW AND TOMORROW

One thing I couldn't stand about grief was the moment I realized Emily would still be dead tomorrow.

Logically, of course, I knew that's what death meant. We're not in the Marvel Comics Universe where caskets come with springboards and you just have to wait a year until your favorite superhero comes back again.

But emotionally, it hit me one day that when Emily should have turned one month old, she'd be dead then too. And on our wedding anniversary, she'd be dead. On my birthday? Yes, even on my birthday. And so on and so forth. In nine years, when she should have put on a white frilly dress and received her First Holy Communion, she wouldn't.

Anniversaries and important dates and would-be milestones? They stank. It felt like no one else even knew about them, and this contributed to the feeling I had that everyone else was moving forward while I stood stuck and unchanging.

WHY YOU MAY FEEL OUT OF PLACE AT INFANT LOSS GROUPS

I attended a real-life in-person infant loss support group for several sessions, but it wasn't quite what I wanted it to be. While I encourage you to look into a local support group, you might not feel like you fit in at first, especially if the group is full of women whose losses are recent.

(This group didn't seem to have "regulars," and maybe other groups have a different dynamic.)

We'd go around the table and share our stories, and the women would be heartbroken, of course, and filled with questions and pain, but what struck me every time was how every one of them was surprised.

And me: I wasn't surprised. I'd been warned, and I'd prepared, and I'd planned, and I'd lived for five and a half months with questions I could turn over in my head at my leisure. They'd come around the table to me, and I sounded like the most heartless woman on the planet because not only was I not in tears, but I actually looked kind of calm.

Once again, for the same reason the bereavement nurses may not have helped you as much as they wanted, you may find you don't quite fit in with the other bereaved moms. It's not your fault. It's just the way things shook out. But looking around the table, I suddenly realized all the pain of the past five months...in a way that had helped. It had helped me to have had the gift of time, and the ability to separate the loss from the questions.

YOU LOOK LIKE YOU HAVE IT ALL TOGETHER

This leads to another issue: everyone looks at you and thinks you have it all together. Your plans have all clicked into motion, and everything worked kind of the way it had to work. There's no frenzy, and you even had a black dress that fit a body you barely recognized.

You're still numb when the funeral happens. You're still in a state of physical shock and emotional exhaustion. People see the brave face and congratulate themselves that everyone's sympathy has supported you. The casserole or the flowers have saved the day.

Within a week, the support dries up. I felt sad when the torrent of sympathy cards dried up. Twenty-one cards one day. Seven cards. One card. No cards.

(Just today, literally today on the day I'm writing this section, someone told me she burst into tears while talking to an acquaintance, and the acquaintance was surprised that she was still sad. "But that was last week!" the woman said, leaving me to wonder whether she's ever endured a tragedy worse than needing to freshen up a houseplant.)

After a week or two, one wants to know any longer if there was anything they could do. And at the point where the numbness and the shock wore off, so have everyone else's thoughts. For me, it was a really lonely feeling. They were on to the next thing, and there I was, standing still.

You might need to remind them that they've moved on to the next thing, but you haven't. And that's fine. A survey of Americans showed that the majority think two weeks is enough time to get over a loss. Nope. Infant loss takes a full two years. Two years. And the grief doesn't peak at the time of the funeral, either.

THE PEAK OF LOSS

On the Carrying to Term support group, we found something odd. Odd in the same way it feels odd to be the only woman in a real-life support group who wasn't caught by surprise.

For us, the peak of loss always seemed to come at three to four months postpartum. We never figured out why, but one after the next we'd experience the same sort of pattern. The numbness after the loss, followed by many horrible days. Then somewhere in there, a good day.

The good day would always be a bit of a shock, and some of us would even feel guilty. How could we dare feel...*good*? Did that make us awful parents?

Well, then there would come more horrible days, so no, it didn't. And then there would be another good day, and then other good days. Eventually the good days would outnumber the bad ones, and we'd hit a stasis.

But the central point in there, the turning point, was the three- to four-month mark, which seemed to be the darkest days, the time when it seemed like nothing would ever change, and everything was and always would be awful.

Maybe it was that three months is about enough time for a woman's body to heal after childbirth. Maybe it's that three months brings you to about the same time of year that a full-term infant would have been conceived. Maybe at three months the brain finally figures it's time to get back to normal, only when it looks around, normal is the furthest thing from possible.

Hang in there through this. There's light ahead. You'll reach it.

MEMORIAL IDEAS

After the birth and death of your baby comes the longest part of the process. I am not an expert on grieving, but those who are say it takes two years to fully come to terms with the death of a baby. I have come to believe the key to a proper acceptance of the death is learning to remember our babies and incorporate them into our souls now that we can't incorporate them into our daily lives. Everyone will accomplish this differently, and everyone will make various steps at his or her own pace. I merely share some of what I did in the hopes that it will give you ideas for memorializing your own child.

OBITUARY

This will be the first memorial for your baby, but unfortunately obituaries for babies are short and don't say much. Longer-lived persons will have their interests and possibly their cause of death listed, but in many communities the obituary for a baby says little more than "infant son of" and a list of surviving relatives.

It pays to think in advance about whether you want a cause of death listed. We didn't consider it until afterward, and I regret that.

They also put only Emily's middle initial in the heading rather than writing out her full name. Since many newspapers print obituaries for free, you may not have much bargaining room, but if something seems important to include, ask for it. The worst that can happen is they refuse because it's not the newspaper's protocol.

BIRTH ANNOUNCEMENTS

We had professional birth announcements printed by a local copy shop that also does engraved wedding invitations. It's a sweet little announcement with a subdued image of a ribbon-heart in a mother-of-pearl color with baby footprints in the middle.

(Note that in order to find this sweet little announcement, we had to page through fifty samples of joyously unbridled-with-delight birth announcements. It's harder to find subdued and stately.)

The copy (in lavender) reads the names of myself, my husband, and my son, and adds that we are "both proud and sad to announce the birth and death of Emily Rose." We then give her time of birth and time of death, and at the bottom the name and address of the charity to which memorial donations could be made in her name.

PHOTOGRAPHS

If you were able to get photographs of your baby, this is the most basic memorial at your disposal. The photos may be very painful to you at first. I am able to pinpoint exactly when Emily died in the procession of photographs because that's when her bear was moved onto my lap with her.

I found it helpful to put all the photos of Emily and Emily's funeral into one photograph album. (Yes, actual printed photos! Even in the digital age, I suggest doing the same for the tactile feel. You want something you can hold.) We chose a decorative album that's no larger than the size of the photos themselves and holds approximately a hundred. There's a space on the metal front for a photo there as well. It looks pretty, and it can stay on display.

There were some photos that didn't fit in this album, and they're in another album of the same type but without the metal frame on the front. I put an angel sticker on that album and keep it with the first. At first I disliked how this isolates her photos from the rest of the family's photos, but on the other hand, if I wanted to look just at her, it was easier to do it. And yeah, duplicate photos? They're our friends.

Speaking of duplicates, I printed copies of every single photograph for all of Emily's grandparents. (Remember, this was seventeen years ago. I didn't get a digital camera until the end of the next year.) This gave the grandparents some measure of inclusion in Emily's memory, and it also gave me peace of mind: four entire houses would have had to burn to the ground simultaneously before all those photos were destroyed.

Nowadays, you'll want to upload the photos to at least two online services for digital storage too. When all you have as a memory is photos, the prospect of their loss becomes vaguely paralyzing. Before we got the copies made, I insisted on bringing Emily's photos with us on long trips just in case something happened to the house.

We made enlargements of some of the photos, framed them, and put them up on the living room wall and mantle beside the rest of our framed photographs. Emily is a part of our family, and I feel best including her there.

VIDEO

The video of Emily's life is too painful for me to watch. I keep the SVHS tapes in her memory box (remember, no digital back then!) and I have one VHS copy in SP mode which we later digitized and stored in several places.

It took years until I felt ready to even try doing anything with that video, even capturing the nicer screenshots. I really wanted to set part of the video to music, but…I can't. I even know which song I'd use, and I can't bring myself to do it.

She's realer in video than in photography, and it feels as though I'm with her there. She made little sweet sounds, and I can hear myself talking to her. It doesn't help that the tape runs out on almost exactly the minute she dies.

Having said that, if you can get video, I think you should. You'll only have one chance to get video, so take advantage of that.

SCRAPBOOK

O you talented scrapbookers! Originally I had intended to make duplicates of all Emily's photos and create a scrapbook the way the proficient crafters can. I imagined I could use photo-corners, stickers, craft paper, etc., to tell her story in more attractive fashion than just a procession of photos in an album.

I've reached the conclusion that when it comes to scrapbooking, I'm an excellent novelist. Emily will just have to reconcile herself in eternity that she's not getting a scrapbook. (*I love you, sweetie, but sorry.*)

There isn't any limit, however, to what *you* could conceivably put in one of these albums. Your child's hospital bracelet, the birth and death certificates or certificate of stillbirth, cards from any flowers you received after your announcement of being pregnant or after your child's death, the prayer card from the funeral, a baptismal certificate, congratulations cards and condolence cards from either end of the pregnancy, and if you happen to have it, your pregnancy test.

The more you think about it, the more you could include. Ribbons from the casket or extra baby socks you never got to use, gifts from friends, a scrap of baby's blanket: they can all go in. Poems or prose pieces (your own or someone else's) that you associate with the grief process can help give structure to your scrapbook. Virtually anything that's flat and reminds you of your child can make a good addition!

My husband has compiled a scrapbook for his youngest brother, since his death came three months after Emily's. My husband said he found the process therapeutic, and he feels good having many memories of his brother all in one place.

FLOWERS

We didn't get very many flowers because we spread the word that we didn't want them. Those we did receive I made sure to dry before they wilted.

Drying flowers is very easy (you probably guessed that already, since I was able to manage it). The basic flower-drying trick is that when they begin to wilt, but before they fall to pieces, suspend them upside-down in a cool, dry, dark location. This way the stems will dry straight.

I tie a thread around the stem and hang it from a nail in my kitchen. Craft stores sell something like hair spray that helps the flower retain its shape. Craft stores also sell a gel that can be added to the water in the vase while the flowers are hale and beautiful, and that will help them retain their color and shape. I have never tried this. I did save the ribbons and cards that came with the flowers.

Once the flowers dry, someone who possesses the elusive crafty instinct, a grape-vine wreath, and a glue-gun can create a flower-wreath out of the dried funeral flowers. Craft stores will have all the necessary materials and may teach classes on the subject.

Some of Emily's flowers were varieties that do not dry well at all. I stripped the petals from those and put them into one of the ubiquitous (and useless) crystal bowls we received for our wedding. They're now in our china cabinet.

For Catholics, there are individuals out there who will take your dried flowers and turn them into rosary beads. We ordered a couple, and the process seems to be that they grind up a few dried flowers and mix them into clay, which they turn into beads and then join into a rosary chain. If this is important to you, get recommendations. We liked the idea, but the ones we ordered didn't turn out very nicely. Some people are wild about theirs, though, so it was probably just bad luck.

DONATIONS

If you select a charity for memorial donations, you can mention it in both the birth announcement and the obituary. This is the one etiquette exception about asking for gifts.

When an adult or a child dies, generally the benefitting charity is one either relating to the cause of death or to a cause the deceased loved, but our babies won't have had causes they loved. Some suggestions would be, therefore, support organizations specific to your baby's condition or doing research into your baby's condition. It could be a generalized infant loss group or a perinatal hospice. You could choose an organization that specifically helped you such as Now I Lay Me Down to Sleep. You could direct donations to your hospital's NICU.

If you want to be creative with your memorial donations, do so! The most memorable donation I've heard of was the family requesting donations in their baby's name be sent to the children's section of their community library. Every so often they still find books with book plates naming their son as the memorial donor.

We chose Birthright, a crisis pregnancy center for which we both worked during college, as the beneficiary. They sent us a list of names as people donated (but not dollar amounts) and we sent the donors thank-you notes in addition to the official ones from Birthright.

If you wish to keep it private, you can still make a donation in your own child's name to a cause you feel worthy of being associated with your little one.

GARDENS

My father and I both started memorial gardens, although mine was the kind that came in a bag with its own fertilizer and a preselected set of wild flowers.

My father's was very elaborate, with flowers and shrubs carefully selected for various reasons. By a string of wild coincidences, he found an Emily Rose aucuba bush, and now he has two of those in his garden. The next year, we were both able to obtain Emily rose bushes. My father's garden has a birdbath statue of an angel. He said it helped him to create the garden and to enjoy the flowers.

CORNER SHELF

I jokingly refer to the corner shelf as The Shrine, and it's devoted to Emily's memorabilia. I had purchased the shelf shortly after we moved into our house, but only after Emily died did my husband finally install the thing.

It's near our wall of photos so that when more photos are added, the shelf will seem like an extension of the family photos. On the shelf we have two small photos of Emily, a teddy bear that arrived in one of her flower arrangements, and an angel from another one. There's a crystal cross from one of Emily's grandmothers, the crucifix laid on her casket during the funeral, and two silk daisies from our church's candle-lighting memorial service for all the deceased.

Above the shelf on the wall we have a framed copy of Emily's footprints (with a lock of her hair), a framed birth announcement, a ceramic cross from my brother and his wife, and the ceramic mold of Emily's feet.

It helps me to have many of Emily's mementos in one location. While I joke about The Shrine, I feel the corner shelf is a means of carving out a space for my daughter among the clutter of our daily lives.

MEMORY BOXES

We have three memory boxes, and they're all full. The first is a sewing box with a pretty pattern on the outside. I bought that at a craft store before her birth to keep all her outfits in until they were needed. Currently it has the outfits sealed in plastic bags, a silk envelope containing a lock of her hair, several smaller gifts from relatives (like a pin and a rosary bracelet), and one of her hospital blankets (again, sealed in a plastic bag.)

(Why sealed in a plastic bag? Because if there's any of her scent left on those items, I want it to stay there. I want to think in my heart of hearts that if I opened up that bag and inhaled, I'd smell her again, the amniotic fluid and the chrism and the sweetness of her newborn self.)

The second is a handsome, dark-wood jewelry box with an engraved nameplate. In this I keep paper mementos, such as her birth and death certificates, obituaries, church bulletins with her name in it, and my pregnancy journal.

The third is a hand-painted wooden box from the hospital, donated for bereaved mothers by a local crafter who herself suffered a neonatal loss. In this I keep some of Emily's things from the hospital: the hats she wore, still with her blood on them (also in plastic bags), the socks she never got to wear, her hospital bracelets and mine, and the SVHS tapes.

Looking through the memory boxes is hard; looking at the items she actually wore or touched is hardest of all.

THE CEMETERY

If you've chosen burial or to bury your baby's ashes, you will have a special place to go for remembering, in addition to any space you may carve out as a memorial spot in your home or garden. If your cemetery permits you to keep long-term decorations at the site, you will have another way to remember your child.

In addition to laying down cut flowers at the grave (carnations last longest, for what it's worth) we have left pinwheels, planted flowers and ivy, left a cute six-inch-tall scarecrow, and placed two Kevlar helium balloons-on-a-stick. (Not all at the same time.)

The balloons are an interesting conundrum, by the way, because many places no longer carry small balloons in a solid color: they have to have a message or a character shape. Before we found anything that would work, we had to root through a lot of "Get Well Soon," "Congratulations!" and "Glad You're Here."

The first suitable balloon we found was a subdued pink with a teddy bear and the words, "Lovely Baby Girl." I affixed that balloon on very tightly and stuck it hard into the ground. When we returned, the stick remained but the balloon was gone. I like to think Emily took it and it's on a mantelpiece in heaven. (Don't laugh. I've had something else taken under circumstances that would make your hair stand on end.) The next time we found a balloon, it was

Winnie-the-Pooh, and this remained all summer until we took it home at the beginning of leaf-blowing season.

For Christmas, we planted a "living tree" from the grocery store (to be uprooted in January when we discovered that "living tree" is a misnomer). We have a flower-fairy garden statue currently. This sounds like a lot, and if it were all on the grave simultaneously it would look like a carnival sideshow. We tried to keep it to three mementos at a time.

Emily's next-door neighbor had a display of silk flowers, a votive light with a candle that can burn for a week at a time, and a Matchbox car (he would have been four). Both that grave and a neighboring grave had stone angel statues. Two others had only annual flowering plants beside the stone, and the remaining three had nothing at all. Any level of decoration depends on you and your preferences, and how you feel most comfortable remembering your baby.

In the beginning, I visited Emily's grave five times a week. As time went on, I visited less frequently (winter cold had something to do with this, as well as progression toward a state of acceptance). I used to visit with my coffee in the morning and linger a long time talking to her.

I've heard from mothers in which the opposite was true: at first they did not want to visit the grave at all, and later they could only as they progressed in their grieving. As in many other cases, whatever level is comfortable to you is fine, even if you never visit. Some families travel to the gravesite on special occasions and spend a couple of hours having a picnic. One woman had a picture taken at the grave with all her living children, in lieu of a family portrait. Whatever significance you want to attach to the gravesite is up to you.

TATTOOS

My sister-in-law Jean came up with an interesting memorial idea for her youngest brother:

I am now the proud owner of a new tattoo! This is not just any tattoo. This is in memory of Chris. I've been wanting another for quite some time and with everything that's happened this, to me, was the perfect idea.

It's on my right shoulder and isn't very big. I'd say about 2"x3" at the most. It's done completely in black but not jet black. It's shaded in different degrees so I guess you could say it's actually kind of gray. It's a dragon wrapped around a sun with a Chinese symbol in the middle of the sun. Basically, it's a dragon with a sun for its tummy.

Now all of this is naturally symbolic. The Chinese symbol is for younger brother. (No real reason why I picked Chinese—it just looked cool to me!) The dragon is because this year is the Chinese year of the Golden Dragon. Which I thought was a unique way to remember the year in which he passed. The Chinese symbol being in the middle of the sun represents how Chris is still surrounded by the family and always will be part of us. The burning flame of the sun represents the love that we have for him. And just like the sun, our love will never be extinguished. It will burn brightly for years to come.

I got the tattoo on my shoulder so I can see it. Every time I look at it I will be reminded of Chris and hope that he somehow approves or at least understands. Just like I hope all the rest of you do.

Jean adds that tattoos hurt and are permanent, so you should think about it for a while before getting it done.

NAMING OPPORTUNITIES

I've lately seen charities selling bricks with names carved into them to be placed on walkways. Emily's name is on at least two of those thanks to my relatives. I've also seen names attached to stained-glass windows, church pews, and the like.

One of the women in my local infant-loss support group had an avid fisherman for a husband. He purchased a new boat in preparation for a fishing tournament about two years after their baby died. He came home one day and said, "I hope you don't mind what I named the boat." He had named the boat after their son. When he went to the tournament, many people asked him why he'd chosen that name, and his wife was surprised to hear him tell their son's story. This was part of the healing process to him.

I have yet to hear of any cars named for children or vanity license plates. You could name your computer or your iPod after your baby, though, and it would be your little secret. Lots of things need names nowadays, so keep an eye out.

WEDDING RING MEMORIAL

Monika of anencephaly.net writes: *After Anouk's death it was important for me to have a sign of her life which I can ever have with me. So I asked a goldsmith to set four small diamonds in my wedding ring. Four diamonds for my four children (Anouk was the fourth). It wasn't expensive at all, since the diamonds are really, really small. I love the idea to have all my family on my wedding ring. The name of my husband inside, the light of my children outside. Today I brought it back to the goldsmith, I wanted him to engrave two little stars inside for the two miscarriages I had before my eldest daughter. Nobody could see these children, not even me, but they are still in my heart. I wanted them to be on my wedding ring too. Only for me. So this wedding ring became a ring of my life.*

LOCK-OF-HAIR LOCKET

Tammy from the support group told us about a locket she got in her daughter Jessica's memory. The locket was designed as a fingerprint locket, but instead she included a small lock of Jessica's hair.

She said the locket was available in lots of places (she got hers at Meijers) and it came with a stamp kit so you could also put your child's fingerprint in it. There were versions in silver and gold for $20 and $40 respectively.

FLOWER ORNAMENTS

Gina from the support group told us about buying clear glass ornaments from a craft store. She'd received numerous flowers from her daughter Christianna's memorial service, so she dried them out. Her idea was to break up the flowers and fill the clear bulbs with the dried petals, then add a bow. She added that she had enough flowers to make ornaments for other family members as well.

CARRYING FORWARD

In the months after Emily's death, I felt rooted to the ground while the world rocketed forward. Everyone else was having babies and watching them grow up while I stayed in place, unchanging. Stuck. When would I have a healthy baby?

THE NEXT BABY

You don't need to make the decision now, but you may want to ask your spouse what he/she thinks is an appropriate period for waiting.

(Your doctor can estimate when you will be physically ready; only you and your spouse can gauge your emotional readiness.)

This may seem like jumping the gun, but if you get yourself through this pregnancy by thinking of another pregnancy six weeks after delivery, and your spouse is thinking eighteen months might be just about enough of a wait, you'll clash when you can least afford to be divided. It's worth it just to know where one another stand.

The one with the shorter timeframe could probably get what he or she wants, but at the expense of marital trust and intimacy. Pick a timeframe you can both live with as a time when you'll discuss it "for real," and reserve the right to change your mind. I know my desire for another child would rapidly fluctuate from "Now! I want one this second" to "Never again in my lifetime."

You'll want to take into consideration your own physical health after delivery, plus anything you may have to do to get your health into good enough shape for another pregnancy. Do you need to supplement with iron or calcium after delivery? If you had a neural tube defect, have you taken folate at the recommended dose for the recommended time?

(Keep in mind that if you wait three months after delivery, you may be conceiving at about the same time of year that the previous baby was conceived, meaning all your milestones may line up on the calendar, and the new baby's due date may be very close to the anniversary of the previous baby's death date. Emotionally, that could be very wrenching.)

When you talk to your health care provider about when you can conceive again, make sure to ask why he or she is recommending the time frame they are. My own midwife said to me, "We tell all our patients to wait a year, but you can probably get pregnant in three months." The general recommendations are considering the average woman who had an average pregnancy and an average delivery. Ask for recommendations based on yourself. If you had an easy delivery and your health isn't compromised, ask your doctor why you would need to wait to conceive again.

You'll especially want to assess your emotional health. While you accept that a new baby will not replace another baby (See our collective rage at Clueless people who toss off a breezy, "You can always have another!"), you may find yourself kind of thinking that the sooner you get started, the sooner you'll have a little one to hold.

Another baby may be a part of your healing, but it can't be the only part. I thought of it this way: it's hard enough going through life as one person. I can't imagine how hard it is to go through life as two people: both yourself and the dead baby you were intended to replace. It might benefit your future baby if you can get some emotional distance between the two. But that's up to you to assess, and then up to you to decide.

FEELING "UNTRUE" TO YOUR LOST LITTLE ONE

Some women have said they couldn't bear to conceive again because they felt they were being untrue to their lost little one. "I wouldn't have had another baby right now if he'd lived. So if I get pregnant right away, I'm pretending he never existed."

If these are your emotions, I'm not going to tell you that they're wrong. But I will reassure you that unlike in a marriage, you never promised any baby would be your one-and-only. Healthy children get younger siblings they didn't want all the time, all over the world. If you're worried that your baby's feelings may be hurt by a future pregnancy, I suggest talking that out with a friend or with your spouse, or even writing a letter to your baby so you can get a better grasp on why you feel that way.

WHY I HATE CALLING IT "TRYING AGAIN"

I find myself chafing when people talk about "trying again." Using the phrase "try again" implies that we failed the first time.

We didn't fail. We had a beautiful baby who happened to have a birth defect that killed her. That's not failure. Loving Emily was a success of a very different kind, and I was glad to have the chance to do so. Emily's life increased my conviction that children are a gift from God, and that I wanted lots of them.

COPING WITH A FOLLOW-UP PREGNANCY

Pregnancy after a loss is like a roller coaster, only you're not sure the seat belt works, you can't see anyone at the control station, and the ride is built over fields of lava. Oh, and there are flaming hoops the cars hurtle through for nine months straight.

Well, maybe it's not quite that bad. But it's...tense.

You've lost your innocence. That's the phrase the moms on the support forums used over and over: "Lost my innocence." "I'm not naive anymore." "I know what can happen."

The day after I got my positive pregnancy test, I looked in the mirror and realized my helplessness. There was nothing I could do to make this pregnancy succeed. Nothing. I couldn't ensure that the baby's chromosomes lined up properly; I couldn't make the embryo implant in the correct part of the uterus; I couldn't close the baby's neural tube. I couldn't do anything important.

I could eat salad and not drink coffee. Pretty much.

Cue forty weeks of tension.

If you hung out on infant loss forums or read infant loss books, you may know far too many ways that a baby can die. I got to the point where I wondered how anybody made it into the world alive.

You'll need to breathe deep and try to trust your body to do its thing. The fact that you cannot control those things means that to some extent, to the best of your power, you'll need to let go of them to keep your sanity.

I looked in the mirror that morning and thought, *I'm not ready to do this again.* When we went for an ultrasound at 22 weeks, I thought, *I'm not ready to do this again.* I just…wasn't ready. I'm not sure how I could have been.

There are support groups geared toward women pregnant again after a loss. (Some people call this their "rainbow baby.") It might be worth looking into one just to reassure yourself that you're not alone.

GOING BACK TO THE SAME HOSPITAL

My midwives usually scheduled the first visit for 8 weeks. When I called, pregnant again after Emily, they said, "How's two o'clock?"

The midwife assessed my emotional state. She can't do anything when the baby's barely implanted, of course. She poked me and said, "That's definitely a pregnant uterus," and I felt better. The majority of the pregnancy care for the next nine months was them dialing back my neuroses.

You'll have to decide whether to stay with the same practice and deliver at the same location. Probably you'll make that decision based on how well or poorly you were treated. If your previous medical provider was a jerk, don't feel any compulsion to stay with that practice. Pick up stakes and move on to the next. And keep moving on if you have to.

The staff at your practice may be genuinely thrilled for you having another baby after they went through your previous pregnancy with you. That's kind of a nice thing. On the flip side, if your pregnancies are close together, you may find you're tired of dealing with the same medical office.

Or this practice may remind you of your previous loss too much, especially if you think they should have done more to help your baby.

Make the decision about which practice you want to go to before you become pregnant. It's easier to choose a new practice before pregnancy than during, and you may want to visit the new practice for a pre-conception consult.

SMELLS, SIGHTS, AND WHY YOU MAY SUDDENLY HATE MATERNITY CLOTHES

You'll find your next pregnancy filled with reminders of the previous one. At every milestone, you may remember exactly what was going on at your pregnancy the last time around.

The first time I walked past an ultrasound room, the smell brought me right back to the ultrasound where Emily was diagnosed. The grief went right through me, and the urge to run. I hadn't thought a smell could do that to me, a smell I hadn't thought of even once in the previous year. But there it was, stored in some brain cells, lurking and waiting to spring out at me. I wasn't even pregnant yet when that happened.

You may find you hate your maternity clothes. I didn't even want to wear maternity clothes again at all when I was pregnant with the next baby. "They're going to have to cut me out of these jeans," I snapped at my husband, who wisely backed off. And when I went for the anatomical scan, I made sure I was wearing nothing I'd worn the previous year when Emily was diagnosed.

Try to keep a good humor about it, is my suggestion. When you catch yourself in an unreasonable emotional reaction, joke about it. ("Yes, Jane, that blue shirt you were wearing at the ultrasound is totally what caused Emily's anencephaly.")

Part of humoring yourself will be going along with whatever tokenism makes you feel better about things, as long as they're not huge issues. Somewhere along the line, I picked up the idea that if someone became pregnant and I bought the baby footwear, the baby would be fine. Everyone who gets pregnant now gets baby socks from me. (I can knit them myself nowadays.) They are my talisman. The only side effect is warm baby feet.

I put off assembling the baby's room until I really couldn't any longer. My husband kept saying, "We need to put up the crib," and I'd reply, "No, we've got time." (He'd glance at the calendar: no, we did not have much time.) But for me, although I'd preplanned everything for Emily, I couldn't bear to preplan anything for the new baby.

Eventually I did wear maternity clothes. I did assemble the crib. And when the time came…I had a baby.

THE FRIENDS AND FAMILY SECTION

If you're here and you're scared, don't worry. You're here for your friend, so I want to say thank you.

In case you jumped directly to this section, I'm going to reiterate something I said in the Clueless chapter: many good-hearted people will say something dumb, and anyone who is sensitive will feel as if she has said something dumb. But for the most part, grieving parents can hear past the fumbling words to the heart.

The defining factor of the Clueless is that they have no heart behind the words. But you're here because you have a heart.

At the same time, hormonal bereaved women aren't known for their good judgment. So let's take a look at how you can help your friends during the worst time of their lives.

IF YOU'RE READING HERE, YOU ALREADY WANT TO HELP, SO YOU PROBABLY WILL

You're doing the most important thing a friend can do for a mother in one of the worst situations imaginable. You're standing at your friend's side, facing into the fire, holding your friend's hand, and just being present. Trust me, that alone is the world.

I'm sure the parents also appreciate your taking the time to do some investigation on their behalf. Several of my friends went web-hunting for sites on anencephaly, helping me screen out the pages with scary photos and reassuring me there was nothing horrible or crude on certain pages.

Through this book, I've said that for the parents, Rule One is "love your baby." For you, Rule One is to love your friend.

There's so little a friend can do in these circumstances. You can't take away the pain. You can't offer an easy way out. By being a friend, you're going to have to suffer right through the baby's pregnancy and death along with the parents. But I found the magic was, those friends who accepted that they couldn't make it any easier *did* make it easier. They did it just by virtue of being there.

They listened. They offered practical help. They looked out for my needs. See? That's your Rule One. Love your friend in whatever way you've become accustomed to, and in whatever way your friend needs right then.

If you jumped right to this chapter, rest assured that nothing in this book is for-parents-only or for-grandparents-only. Look through everything. Absorb whatever information you can and figure out how best you can help.

If you're pre-reading to screen this book for a friend, even once you've determined that there's "nothing scary" here, you may want to look over the issues the parents will face or are facing in order to prepare yourself for what will come. Then you will know in advance about the difficult shopping trips or anniversaries, and you'll know what they might need.

If you're here because you don't know what to do, I know what I wanted from my friends, and I know that most of them gave it to me. I wanted them to follow my cues and talk about Emily with the same freedom I did. I wanted them to laugh at my gallows humor even if they weren't sure it was entirely polite to laugh. (Well, I wasn't sure it was entirely okay to joke around.) I wanted them to check up on me from time to time, and then when they knew I was going to the hospital, I wanted them to call for information and not mind when I didn't feel up to talking to them.

Afterward, I wanted their presence at the funeral. I wanted sympathy cards. I wanted them to tell me what reminded them of my daughter. I wanted them to listen. I wanted them to ask about her photographs and I wanted them to come to the gravesite with me.

But what to do? All the nebulous offers of "If there's anything I can do" meant very little to me. In the middle of chaos, I found it impossible to find something for the well-wishers to do. My suggestion is to take the reins and offer something specific.

The best idea I've ever heard is sending the family a gift certificate to their favorite pizza place that delivers, or any service that delivers food.

A QUOTE ABOUT RULE ONE

"When we honestly ask ourselves which persons in our lives mean the most to us, we often find that it is those who, instead of giving much advice, solutions, or cures, have chosen rather to share our pain and touch our wounds with a gentle and tender hand. The friend who can be silent with us in a moment of despair or confusion, who can stay with us in an hour of grief and bereavement, who can tolerate not knowing, not-curing, not-healing and face with us the reality of our powerlessness, that is the friend who cares."

-Henri J.M. Nouwen, "Out of Solitude" (as quoted in *Pregnancy after a Loss*)

MEMENTOS TO GIVE THE PARENTS

If you like to give "stuff," the easiest thing in the world is a memento for the baby.

Except, of course, that it's the hardest thing in the world because you may find yourself standing in the store looking at all these things and thinking, "None of this will make any difference." Be brave. Your friend understands this. But your gift may be the one she treasures forever, so take a deep breath.

I would suggest not giving something that would be perceived as "useful." I trembled at the thought of receiving outfits Emily would never wear.

But a picture frame? A memory box? Those were very much appreciated. A journal. A stuffed animal.

The stuffed animal who serves as a stand-in for Emily in all our photos was a gift from a relative. So was the mother-and-baby necklace I wore in her memory.

If you can knit, crochet, or quilt, it will hurt like blazes, but you might be able to make something for the baby. (If you make a hat, be warned that anencephalic babies will have impossibly tiny heads.) A blanket or a handmade stuffed animal may be just right for your friend to cuddle in the days leading up to the birth or in the lonely aftermath.

Other people have told me they've received care packages of non-perishable foods, grief books, silly gifts that had nothing whatsoever to do with grieving, and long letters from their friends that they could keep in their memory book.

USING THE BABY'S NAME

The biggest gift you will give your friend is treating your friend's baby like a person who matters.

To that end, please us the baby's name. It has always shocked me how people are afraid to say the name of someone who's died. Go ahead and say the name, even if it feels uncomfortable at first.

DATES, ANNIVERSARIES, THINGS THAT WILL NEVER HAPPEN

Think about the time markers involved in a healthy baby's earliest days. "He's two weeks old." "She's one month old."

After the baby's death, the parents are still marking time in the same way, only it's "should have been." This should have been her due date. He should have been one week old. She should have turned one month old today.

I know this is hard because it's not intuitive, but please try to reach out to the parents on those days. Mark them on your calendar if you have to, but please try to remember the monthly anniversaries, at least for the first six months.

I was surprised by how many people called on Emily's one-year anniversary, some without ever saying why. They just coyly…called. Or asked if I wanted to go to lunch.

But we also got some cards expressly remembering her on her first birthday, and seventeen years later, I still get messages from some relatives and family friends on Emily's birthday.

We want to know our babies will be remembered, and who better to remember our babies than our best and closest friends?

THE WORLD'S BEST POTATO SALAD

I'm not from the South, so this whole "casserole after a death" thing took me by surprise the first time I saw it in action. One family had two refrigerators overfull with casseroles, fruit, a cake, and two dozen eggs that a friend had collected from her chickens that morning.

When Emily died (in New England), there were no casseroles. We catered the lunch after the funeral by ordering trays of lunch meat and bags of rolls from BJ's Wholesale. But then a friend rang the doorbell, and she, my dear reader, was from the South.

She brought me the largest potato salad I had ever seen in my life, and ever since too. "I knew you had guests, so I thought you'd want to feed them."

I could have had all of Brooklyn, NY for guests with this potato salad. I hugged her and thanked her and cried, and tucked the potato salad into the fridge. I felt kind of bad because she'd put in so much work, and I don't like potato salad.

When we ate, I dutifully ladled some onto my plate with the lunch meat and the roll, and you know what? It was the world's best potato salad. I had no idea potato salad could taste that good.

You know what made it so good? The fact that she cared that I should eat even though my baby was dead. She cared enough that she wanted to make sure I was fed. Food is love. That's true in Italian households like mine, and it's true in the South as well. Food is love, and by peeling a thousand pounds of potatoes and cooking them and chopping up a red onion and adding mayo and dill relish, she'd also ended up adding a big heaping spoonful of love.

If you bring food, your friend will taste the love.

But be creative and expand this idea out into other areas: be practical. Maybe she needs her laundry folded before the guests come, or maybe he needs help finding funeral shoes for the other kids, or maybe the baby's grandmother needs a ride from the airport. If you can anticipate the need and meet it, your friend will know and appreciate your love.

THE SPONTANEOUS WATERWORKS MACHINE

I hope you're comfortable with tears.

Some professional a very long time ago told me that it's considered a bad thing in therapy to hand your patient a box of tissues. "It means you're ashamed of their tears," the professional said by way of explanation.

I have no idea if this is true, but I do know Americans are profoundly uncomfortable with crying. It's bad enough when women cry, but men crying? We don't know what to do about it.

Well, if a baby's death or impending death isn't worth crying over, nothing is. The parents need to cry. Crying is healthy. Crying is healing.

It's okay if you cry too.

It's okay to reach across the table and hold your friend's hand and just sit in silence while he or she cries. It's okay to hug and just sit in silence. You're not being asked to stop the tears. It's not your fault that the tears started, even if they started after something you said or did.

I called myself the Spontaneous Waterworks Machine. Hey, it happens. And it will probably happen again too.

WHY NOT TO WORRY ABOUT SAYING STUPID THINGS

The two concerns I hear most often from friends are these:

"I don't want to remind her"

and

"I don't want to say the wrong thing."

Let's put the first one to rest right now: you aren't reminding your friend either that the baby died or that the baby is going to die. Your friend is already thinking about it. You might think your friend is thinking about cooking or driving or whatever other thing it is you're talking about, but for the next year or so, your friend is thinking about the baby. You can't remind your friend in a world already full of reminders.

The second one is trickier because we all know about the horrible and mean things people say when they hear about a death. "It's better this way." "At least you can have another." "Other people have it worse." "You wouldn't have loved a monster like that anyhow." "What did you do to cause this?"

The common thread among horrible things people say is that the speaker wants to shut down the other person's grief and sadness. Genuine grief makes the speaker uncomfortable, and therefor the speaker blames the griever for that discomfort. Hence words of "comfort" and "wisdom" that come off like an attack. Why? Because they are.

You're not going to do that because you have a heart

If you don't know what to say, still say something. Anything is better than nothing.

Even if you don't know how to feel, the parents in trouble still need to know they have supportive friends who care about them and who won't vanish when they're in need.

You want a simple formula? "I'm so sorry to hear about your baby's diagnosis."

There you go. You're not ashamed of their baby's diagnosis. You are acknowledging it and the pain they feel.

"I can't imagine how awful it feels."

And then, depending on your religious beliefs, you might add, "I'm praying for you" or "I'm thinking about you."

That's shorthand for "Well crud, I have no idea what to say."

Your words don't have to be poetic or pain relieving. You're not going to win a Pulitzer Prize for your message, nor does anyone expect you to. All the grieving parents want to hear is that you are there for them. Rule One for you: you're still going to be their friend.

We received a number of confused (and confusing) emails after we spread word of the diagnosis. They were all heartfelt, and I appreciated the genuine fumbling regardless of anyone's level of eloquence.

Don't worry about saying the "wrong" thing. The only wrong thing is silence.

A FEW THINGS PLEASE NOT TO SAY

Having said that the only wrong thing is silence, I'd like to make a suggestion please.

Please don't say the words "at least."

"At least" is an attempt to alleviate the grieving parent's pain, and we get it, you don't want us to be hurting. But it never helps as much as people think.

"At least you can have another baby" just brings the parent to the thought that they're losing the baby they love right now, and then the horrible question: what if they can't ever have a healthy baby? What if they can't bear to go through this again?

Now if the parents say "at least" and are looking for a silver lining, go ahead and agree with them. Sure, at least you found out now rather than being surprised at the birth. But the silver lining is for them to find, not for you. Right now, just acknowledge.

If you must use "at least" in a sentence, let it be more along the lines of, "This is a terrible situation, but at least let me vacuum for you before your mother-in-law gets here."

SO THERE YOU HAVE IT

You're in one of the most difficult jobs in the world. I don't envy you. In retrospect, I felt really bad for my friends because of how big our situation was, and how little any of us could do to influence it.

But if you've read this book, you might have noticed something: how often I mention little things my friends did. None of their actions made newspaper headlines, but they're peppered all over the place: *I came and taught her a few guitar chords. I made her a potato salad. I read a few websites and was able to talk to her about what would happen afterward. I bought her a mother-and-child necklace.*

Could I have done it without them? I don't think so. On the days when I doubted I could get from breakfast time to lunch time, there was always this chorus of voices offering encouragement and understanding. I was on the battlefront, but they had my back. Even if they could only offer agreement, they were offering something.

This is where the rubber meets the road. This is where you're showing the strength of your friendship to someone who has no strength of her own.

Losing a baby is one of the loneliest roads in the world. Imagine yourself at your friend's side at the trailhead, looking up the mountain at a path that twists around boulders and runs between ditches. Your friend's backpack weighs twenty-five pounds, and she can't put it down. You've gotten a look at the map and there isn't even a scenic overlook.

Still, you cut each of you a tough branch and test them out as walking sticks. You offer to carry her water bottle, and you put your hand on her shoulder.

"Are you going that way?" you say. She nods, and you answer, "Then I'm going there too."

It's all you can do. But it's the best thing anyone can.

THE CAREGIVER SECTION FOR PROFESSIONALS

The first book I read on infant loss said that the first fifteen seconds after a loss determines whether an obstetric patient remains with their provider. While that might be an exaggeration, it's not an exaggeration to say that medical caregivers have a huge impact on how the parents perceive their pregnancy.

You as a medical care provider, whether as a doctor, a nurse, a therapist, a genetic counselor, or what-have-you, are in a position of authority. You can use your authority to help the parent follow what I've been calling Rule One throughout the book. Rule One is "Love your baby." Your professional Rule One is to use your authority to help the parents do right by their baby.

If you are a medical professional who wants to learn more about support after infant loss, I highly recommend Gary Vogel's A Caregiver's Handbook to Perinatal Loss *and Limbo & Wheeler's* When a Baby Dies. *Both have good and compassionate suggestions of things to say, do, and avoid.*

RESPECT FOR THE PARENTS AND THEIR DECISION

The number one complaint on the Carrying to Term forums is that their doctors don't respect the parents' decision to go to term.

Disrespect manifests in any number of ways. If you read my daughter's story, think about the doctor who accosted us after the diagnosis. She lied to me. She told me worst-case scenarios that could only happen with shoddy medical care but implied they would happen to me if we didn't terminate. She was rude about my baby and then acted condescending to me.

She actually said, "You won't remember a word of this conversation tomorrow."

I remember it all. I assure you. I remember every lousy word that came out of her mouth.

Contrast to the midwives I went back to afterward. Every one of them hugged me. Sure, they hedged their support ("We know you made the best decision *for you*") but never did they question my sanity or my intelligence. Never did they call my baby ugly. When I told them the doctor had said (and yes, this is a direct quote) "Just because you feel the baby moving doesn't mean it's alive," they responded in horror and disbelief.

Disrespect comes in talking down to the patient. It comes in reminding her that whatever she's asking about "won't make any difference," as though she's forgotten her baby will die. Disrespect can take the form of a recoil on opening the exam room door and finding the mother still there, still pregnant. Disrespect can take the form of asking at every single appointment if the mother has changed her mind about carrying the pregnancy to term.

If a doctor or other caregiver truly can't respect the parents' decision, then the caregiver should do them the respect of referring them to another medical professional.

Respect looks like treating the pregnancy in many ways like other pregnancies, doing the same routine care and making the same kinds of observations.

Respect looks sometimes like treating the pregnancy differently, scheduling more frequent appointments or longer ones.

Respect looks like being proud of this baby the same way you're proud of all the healthy babies.

Respect means agreeing that you can't save the day, but you can help the parents salvage whatever they can.

Respect means listening, means acknowledging, means being fully present. Respect means looking at these parents and remembering you went into medicine because you wanted to help people, and here are two people who need your help.

TREATING THE PREGNANCY THE SAME AS ANY OTHER PREGNANCY

I'm about to be contradictory, but that's okay. Bereaved moms are allowed to be contradictory. Pregnancy is all about giving life, and instead this is all about death, so that's a contradiction right from the get-go.

After the diagnosis, you should as much as possible treat the pregnancy like any other pregnancy.

If you would pull out the heartbeat monitor at every appointment, continue to do so. If you would take fundal height and palpate the baby's position, continue to do so. Glucose challenge test? Offer it the way you always offer it.

Follow your practice's protocols as much as they make sense. As one midwife told me, "Emily's condition is no reason to provide shoddy medical care."

The mother will derive some comfort in continuing to see you and being treated similarly to other mothers. If anything, she'll find her visits more intense and more memorable because they're part of a very small pool of memories she'll have for her baby. If she's already had a baby, she'll know and expect the routines and the milestones. If she hasn't, then you're helping her chart new territory, and you're doing it at her side. She's going to appreciate that.

...EXCEPT WHEN YOU DON'T

And then the contradiction: sometimes it's best to treat this mother and this pregnancy differently.

This mother may not explicitly require more appointments, but maybe she should go to biweekly appointments sooner than usual. Maybe she should have longer appointments.

If you don't routinely offer ultrasounds in the third trimester, maybe the baby's birth defect qualifies for an extra one. Or maybe you could leave the wand on the mother's abdomen just a bit longer, so she can listen to the baby's heartbeat and take courage from that.

Some medical tests or procedures, like the group B strep test, become unnecessary when the baby isn't going to survive. Why subject them to the test and the follow-up when it really will make no difference?

Some mothers have argued against fetal monitoring during labor on the grounds that if a c-section is off the table (since it won't affect the baby's longevity), then they don't want to know if the baby dies during labor. They feel it would be too disheartening and too difficult to push knowing the baby had died. So in those cases, even if your hospital has standing orders for fetal monitoring, this is the time to say no. Or to tell your patient how to refuse consent to something you and she both know she doesn't need.

Speaking of c-sections, some women believe a c-section will give them a higher chance of being able to hold their baby alive after birth. If the mother wants to discuss that with you, look up the statistics for her baby's particular birth defect and what effect the method of delivery has on the baby's longevity. For some, it might not matter at all, so have those statistics on hand. For others, if it does have an effect, you show your respect for the mother's concerns by discussing whether an elective surgical delivery is the best option for her and her baby considering all the circumstances. Even if you wouldn't ordinarily consider an elective surgical delivery, now may be the time to do so. But at least discuss it.

Think about all the routine newborn activities with a hospital. Bend the rules for those. Put that baby right into the mother's arms and let the weighing and measuring and cleaning happen later, if at all. If the baby is going to live for only an hour, it makes no sense for the baby to spend forty-five minutes in a warmer. In fact, it's cruel.

Bending the rules is okay when the rules weren't made for this kind of situation. Sometimes, compassion demands nothing else.

How will you know when it's best to hold to routine and when it's best to jettison? Listening.

LISTENING TO THE PARENTS' LOGIC

I'm pretty sure I sounded insane. When I talked to medical professionals, I had it all straight in my head, but the logic came out all sideways.

About two weeks after Emily's diagnosis, I came down with a horrible ear infection, so I went to my PCP. He peeked in my ear and said yes, otitis media, and started to write a prescription.

But wait, I said. *I'm pregnant.*

So he pulled off the prescription and started writing something else, and I said, *But wait, see, the baby's going to die, so it's not like the antibiotic will hurt her, but I don't want it to hurt her, so if you can give me something that won't hurt her, but it doesn't matter, so if you have to do it—*

If you as a medical professional right now are feeling really awful for the poor man, I assure you that I feel sorry for him as well.

So in this weird, bizarro way I tried explaining to him what was going on (and as opposed to the conversation with that horrible obstetrician, I remember very little of this one) but I do remember one moment with absolute clarity. One incredible, amazing moment that changed the way I looked at this doctor for the next ten years I spent in his practice.

At the very end of my babbling explanation, he handed me the script for an antibiotic, one safe for pregnancy. Then he offered that after the birth, "I could write you a prescription for an antidepressant. Something that acts quickly."

And he looked helpless.

I'd always thought of this doctor as cold, the kind of guy who pictured himself seated atop a mountain, dispensing health. But here I was as an unsolvable problem. The only thing he could do, with years of medical school and residency and practice...the *only* thing he could do...was offer me a medication that might make me feel less sad.

Which I never ended up taking.

The thing is, he listened to me. He heard past the nonsense that came out of my mouth to the major issues: *I needed a medication, and I wanted to advocate for my baby, and I didn't want to cause problems, and the baby was dying, but I was still a mother to her, and I wanted to protect her, and on and on and on.* All that blather, and he heard, "She needs an antibiotic for her ear, and she needs me to care."

You can listen too. Sometimes a parent is going to come to you with a request you consider just short of insane, but listen past that to the logic. Tease out their unspoken assumptions. Yes, for 99% of your clients, you've probably heard it all before, but this situation is the outlier. That means the questions will be outliers as well. The reasons will be outliers. The desires will be outliers.

So ask questions and listen to the answers. What they're asking may make sense once you see the logic behind it.

COMPUTER MODE

As a medical professional, you are trained in recognizing a problem within about a minute, even with incomplete information, and in the next ten seconds settling on a course of treatment. That's an incredible skill, and one you've probably developed under great pressure.

In cases like ours, please make sure you've selected and are treating the right problem.

This works really well...except when it doesn't. Ready?

TARGET: The patient wants me to solve her problem.
DEFINITION: Her problem is that the baby is going to die.
ERROR: I cannot solve this problem.
RETARGET: Create a new problem.
DEFINITION: Problem is that she is still pregnant.
SOLUTION: End the pregnancy.

Please catch yourself between the ERROR and RETARGET phases because once you've redefined the problem that way, your patient becomes your enemy.

Patients get defensive with their care providers in many cases after the care providers have already become defensive with the patients.

You may be dealing with a patient who was previously treated this way, or who was pushed toward termination by a doctor intent on solving the second problem when s/he realized it was impossible to solve the first. Again, get at the patient's logic and hear past the defensiveness. It will take time, but your respectful treatment and your advocacy of the parents' needs is going to wear down their resistance to you.

My PCP couldn't solve the problem of my baby dying (because no one could) so he retargeted and tried to solve the problem of me being sad because she was dying. When I didn't want antidepressants, a lesser professional would have then retargeted the problem this way:

NEW PROBLEM: Patient refuses treatment.

But no, you and your patient are on the same side. They are going to love their baby in whatever time they have. You are going to provide excellent care in whatever time they have. You will look out for the medical aspect of their pregnancy so they can look out for the emotional and relational aspect of their pregnancy.

Grief is the problem, and while you're an expert problem solver, you cannot solve grief.

It's okay that you can't solve this problem. We understand and accept it. While the parents are doing whatever they can, you will be doing whatever you can, and you'll be doing it in conjunction with them rather than at odds with them.

SHOWING VULNERABILITY

Doctors know all the answers, right? And when they don't, they at least can write a referral to someone who does. That's a pretty powerful position. There's skill. There's knowledge. There's a network of professionals in wait to support even the trickiest cases. There are machines and tests, and at the fulcrum you stand, ready to interpret the results.

This holds true to some extent for all the medical professions. You know how the systems operate, and you know how to intervene in a malfunctioning system to get things back on track. Physical or psychological, you've got a degree and certification and experience. You've got this.

But then there's this mother sitting in your office with a problem you can't solve.

She's vulnerable. You want to be strong. We know you want to be strong.

It's okay to be vulnerable. It's okay to let her see your helplessness. The moment I saw my own doctor's helplessness was the moment I changed the way I viewed him and gave me added respect for what a good doctor he was.

I can tell you about the times my midwives cried. I thought better of them for it, not worse.

Showing vulnerability will achieve something else, too: it will give your patients permission to show their vulnerability to you. Being vulnerable together, unafraid of your weakness, is one of the best ways of being together on the same side.

If it happens, it happens. Let your patient know you're all working together, and in some ways, you're equally helpless. You'll leverage your authority on their behalf as much as possible. That's the antidote to computer mode: human mode, heart to heart.

"WARM BLANKET CARE"

The nasty doctor who told me I wouldn't remember any of the details tomorrow didn't realize something you probably do: the details matter.

What you might not realize is how *much* they matter. Remembering details is one of the ways you show you care, but of course simply rememberng them isn't enough. Noticing details and then mentioning them or acting on them is.

Parents always remember the things their doctor forgot. "She forgot I was allergic to penicillin when I'd mentioned it two minutes earlier." "He told me to go home and relax with a funny movie and an ice cream when he knows I'm diabetic. It's right there in the chart."

It's heartening to hear about the things a caregiver remembers, though. "He remembered that she jumps whenever he turns on the Doppler." "She knew before I even reminded her that we were waiting for a call back from the specialist."

Nursing staff who remember small details are the ones who have the most impact. "She remembered I didn't like ice, and for the rest of the hospital stay, every shift put ice in the pitcher, but she didn't."

There's a family story about my grandmother who went to visit her own mother in the hospital. Her mother was crying. The staff wrote off her tears by saying she was drugged and not lucid. My grandmother, however, sat beside her and studied her. She looked her all over, and then she asked for three cotton balls. When the nurses found some for her, she put the cotton balls between my great-grandmother's wrist and the cast she was wearing. The edge of the cast was rubbing a sore on her wrist, and no one had taken the time to notice. To everyone else, this detail wasn't important. To my grandmother it was. And my great-grandmother stopped crying.

That's why I'm calling this part "warm blanket care." A provider walks into the hospital room and is confronted with monitors and readouts and a patient's chart, but what does she do first? She steps outside and gets a blanket from the warmer because the patient is huddled up on the bed, and it matters to her that the patient is comfortable. She takes care of that need first, and then she can go look at the monitors and the chart and the printouts.

Would being slightly chilly in a hospital room kill the patient? Would it affect her outcome? No. But it's worth fixing.

"Warm blanket care" acknowledges that small gestures make a tremendous difference, and that you care enough to notice what needs to be done.

RESPECTING THE BABY

The details matter most when it comes to the baby, and they're also the way you show respect to the baby.

Use the baby's name if you know it. If you don't know it, ask. The parents might think you don't want to know, but you do. Put it in the chart and then refer to the baby by name. "Hey, let's get Jacob's heartbeat."

Remember, they only have nine months max to remember their baby, so the things you say will burn into their memory. "Wow, Ginny's moving a lot today." If you're proud of their baby, they'll have reason to be proud too. "Hey, Alex is right on the growth curve! What a fighter."

Talk to the baby. "Okay, Emily. Which way are you facing today?"

One doctor, after every delivery, would sing, "Happy Birthday to You." If you do something like that after healthy deliveries, try to do it after this baby's delivery as well.

(Presuming there isn't, of course, some kind of mad scramble to get the baby stable. One assumes this doctor doesn't sing "Happy Birthday to You" while racing to the NICU alongside a crash cart.)

If you have a wall of photos, covered in pictures of babies you delivered, ask the parents for a copy of their baby's photo. Display him or her alongside all the healthy babies.

And remember this, because this is what I wrote on the back of Emily's photo that's hanging on the midwives' wall: Anyone can deliver a healthy pregnancy, but it takes star quality to deliver one this difficult.

WHEN IS DEPRESSION JUST HEALTHY GRIEVING, AND WHEN DOES DEPRESSION NEED MEDICATION OR THERAPY?

Well, isn't this the million-dollar question?

Healthy grief is normal and should be supported. Losing a baby is, by definition, "complicated grief," and it will take two years to reach some kind of resolution. Your patient needs to understand that he or she won't be back to normal (whatever that is) in a couple of weeks. No matter what other people expect, it will probably take years, and the worst point will probably be at about the four-month mark.

Patients who are pre-grieving will tackle some of the metaphysical and emotional issues prior to the loss, but they're not going to spring right back to normal. They'll need time and patience. They'll need to talk.

It might be that everyone in that situation would benefit from grief counseling, but of course not everyone will want it. That's fine.

But as doctors, nurses, and therapists, the work is going to be teasing apart what depression is a normal part of grieving, and what depression is a dysfunctional, stalled version of grief.

Some cases will be clear cut. Someone who's thinking of harming herself needs intense medical intervention and needs it now. Someone who's crying every day but is otherwise functioning doesn't need medication but might need a grief counselor.

But then you've got that mother who's not sure. Who's unable to meet your eyes but who seems to be functioning. Who doesn't know if she needs medication. Who can't make up her mind about how bad it really is.

That's tough, and that is why I suggested paying attention to the details. That's why I suggested really listening. Hearing the parents' logic. Getting to know them. Earning their trust. Making sure they know you will advocate for them even if it means making hospital administration angry with you.

Because when you're faced with that tricky situation, with the patient where you're not sure if she's just-enough depressed or *too* depressed, or oddly not depressed at all and in some kind of weird psychological denial…it's going to be the past relationship you built up with that patient that gives you your answer. And it will be the way you've proven yourself that convinces the patient to let you help.

"BE SURE TO BRING YOUR BABY TO THE POSTPARTUM CHECKUP!" AND OTHER UNNECESSARY ROUGHNESS

When I booked my postpartum checkups (two weeks and six weeks, per their protocol for after a loss) I stupidly asked if there was anything special I should bring with me.

The receptionist responded, "Be sure to bring your baby!"

I replied, "Well, she's dead. But I'd like to."

The receptionist probably felt like an idiot for the rest of the month, but I get it. It's autopilot, like the heroic customer service representative who spent twenty minutes rebooking flights for me after my brother-in-law's unexpected death, then finding us a rental car and a hotel *and* getting us a funeral discount, and right before she got off the phone, topped it off by saying, "Have a nice day."

If you're at all like me, you might wake up at three a.m. twenty years later and think, "Gosh, I'm an awful person."

Neither of these are awful people. One of those situations is actually funny. But they're regular people in awful situations, and they went by the script.

If possible, figure out a way to flag a family's chart or folder or computer file in order to prevent slip-ups. If the hospital is supposed to flag the patient's door, please make sure it's flagged. Since you know in advance that this family will be facing bereavement, line things up in advance so the maternity unit has bereavement-trained nurses assigned to them that day, and the social worker or the hospital chaplain know to come up. Intercept the phlebotomy tech or the meal service worker and say, "Hey, keep a low profile in room 115."

If you can schedule the postpartum visit for a time when you normally see gynecological patients rather than pregnant women or postpartum women, that would help. If you can shift the newly delivered mother to the far end of the hallway so she won't hear crying babies, that would help too. Details. So many details, but they make so much difference.

YES, I'M VERY DEMANDING

As it turns out, whether you're a nurse or a doctor or a therapist or what-have-you, these parents are not your only clients. I'm not sure what kind of superhero would be able to pull off all the suggestions I've made in this chapter. All the little things, that is.

Respect and attention? Yes, you can do those things. And that's where you'll succeed and end up on the Gold Star Wall of Fame for your clients. You might miss the detail that the parent is wearing red because her baby's outfit was red and it's a way of being close to her baby. (She probably realizes you aren't a mind-reader.) But your attitude will come through. If you had noticed the red thing, you'd have acknowledged it.

Parents can tell when a doctor or a therapist actually cares. Several years after Emily's death, I had several sessions with a spiritual director (which is like a religious therapist). She was very nice and seemed to have good insight, and after a few sessions, I entrusted her with something very personal. I showed her my vulnerability, and then she...kind of ignored it.

I didn't actively terminate sessions with her. I just never booked another appointment. She wrote me after two months and asked if I was upset because her schedule was busy, and I said no. I wasn't *upset*. But after realizing that I wasn't valued in a relationship where I wanted to be valued, I picked up stakes and quietly disappeared.

I've had professionals give me questionable advice and I've kept going back to them because even if their advice wasn't spot-on, they made it clear they valued me.

This is where I'd like to see you position yourself as a caregiver. Not that you'd give questionable advice, but that when they're telling their baby's story for years to come, or when they're reliving those key moments, or when they pull down the photo album, the parents say, "Oh, So-and-so? They were amazing." Why? Because you listened and responded, you acknowledged and respected.

And when someone new to town says, "Hey, do you have a recommendation?" your name rolls right out of their mouth because you cared.

"She's sharp as a tack," they might say, "and she's not like all the others. She listens to you."

She hugged me.

He called the hospital and told them my baby was not to be taken away from me.

She gave me her cell phone number and said to call her at any time of the day or night.

He had me come back into the office on his lunch hour so I could get the ultrasound pictures they didn't take the first time.

She sang happy birthday to my baby.
He cried with me in the hospital room.
She respected me.
He cared.

See yourself in this scenario. That's you. You're a caregiver. The one who cares is you.

OUR AFTERMATH

Some people say you "get over" your grief. I never found that to be the case. Instead, I call the process "carrying forward." You can move forward with your life, but you're always going to be carrying this experience and this loss within your heart. The burden will ease over time. You'll get used to the weight of the thing, and the pain will be less. Some days you'll hardly notice it at all. But you haven't gotten over it or worked around it. You're carrying it with you.

"HOW MANY CHILDREN DO YOU HAVE?"

This is the worst question on earth because it's so innocent. You'll meet someone at a playground and she tells you her name, then says, "That's my son Jack on the slide." She says she's new in town, and then, "How many children do you have?"

No one means any malice by this. They have no reason to assume it's even an issue, so if they're Clueless, it's an innocent Cluelessness. They're making small talk, only for you it's not so small.

The full answer might be like this: "Well, my oldest is in college now. He's doing great. I've got a daughter who's in high school, and two more sons, one in middle school and one in grammar school. Yeah, they're spaced kind of far apart. And then there's Emily Rose, the one you're not going to see here at any of the school events because she died when she was two hours old. That was lousy. But the rest of our family has kind of taken its shape around her, and if you look closely, you can see the space she would have inhabited."

Instead you say, "Four." Because this is a total stranger.

"I feel like I'm denying my baby's existence," women say on the support forums.

You're free to answer this question however you like, of course. If you want to tell a total stranger about your lost little one, that's your right. Half the time if you do this, the other person will open up and tell you about a miscarriage that only three people know about, or she'll tell you how her sister was infertile for five years.

Suddenly, they trust you. You're safe. You understand their pain, and you led the way for them by being vulnerable.

On the other hand, because some people can respond to your vulnerability by being jerks, you're perfectly entitled to have a "secret baby." They don't need to know. Then, when and if you feel like inviting the person closer into your circle, you can disclose to them as you see fit. They'll know then that this is precious information, entrusted to only the most special people in your heart.

When people make remarks at me about having four children, I do shoot back at them, "These are only the ones I brought with me." And they goggle. I think Emily would approve.

CARRYING FORWARD

We did go on to have three more children.

All three came into the world in the usual way, with their mother kind of stressed and never quite sure everything was going to be okay, no matter how okay everything seemed.

All four living children know about their sister Emily Rose. They talk about her freely with themselves and with one another. They get to decide whether they include her on family tree projects for school.

Emily's shelf is still up in our house, although we've moved to a new house now. We include her in our family portraits by bringing along her stuffed bunny, and every year the bunny gets included in the photos. Only one person has ever asked us about the omnipresent bunny, and when I told him, he said it was a good way to include her. I also wear my mother-and-child necklace.

We've moved away from the city where Emily is buried, but once a year we drive through there, and we stop for a visit. The cemetery is still silent and clean. We leave her a flower or a pinwheel, and we say a prayer.

My second daughter has put together that if Emily had survived, she most likely wouldn't have been conceived.

Emily is her only sister. All the rest are boys, and sometimes people say they feel sorry for her being the only girl in the house. She lets it slide.

Sometimes I've felt Emily's presence in the house. Sometimes I've smelled the chrism from her hair in the hair of my other babies, and one time, I handed the baby to my husband, and he smelled it too. "It's 18 months," he said. I hadn't realized the date until he said it.

I haven't seen her in dreams, but I've had other experiences where I know she's been active.

I like to think that her life was a complete fulfillment of what could have been. We loved her as much as we could for the brief time we had her. We carried her story out into the world, and her life touched others. Changed others. Changed us. And we carry those changes forward even when the grief no longer flattens us down.

HELPING OTHERS

What I settled on in the long run was that I wanted Emily's life to help others. That's where I was going to find meaning in what we'd endured.

Helping others wouldn't make things right, but I felt it would at least give a purpose to the pain. So I reached out and tried to help others, or at least be there for them, as a means of healing my own broken heart.

The thing about drowning is that two drowning people can't pull each other to shore. That's why a support group is so useful: people are all at different stages of the journey.

For a while I absorbed their help; later I became a source for it. At my worst points, still I could listen and agree. One day, I posted in the group, "Grieving sucks." That's it, nothing more, and a dozen replies came back to me: *Yes, it does. Yes. Yes, amen.*

But over time I realized something else was taking place: parenting Emily hadn't just made me some kind of helpful person. Parenting her had changed me. I listened better. I learned more. I knew my own weakness. I'd learned to accept help and say "Thank you," which you know is hard when you're an overfunctioner and planner and someone who really likes control. I'd learned to let my friends be a friend to me when I had nothing to offer them.

I'd learned to be vulnerable. Remember when I said to the nurse, "I probably have eighty years to live, but she's only got five months." What if Emily changed me such that her effects were going to be felt not just for those five months, but for the rest of those eighty years?

What if she changed the way I parented her siblings? What if that changes the way her siblings eventually parent their own children?

What if I was always going to be a little bit sadder, a little bit more understanding, a little bit more patient? What if I was going to have a better perspective on what mattered? What if I'd become the kind of person that people told their secrets to while standing in a McDonalds PlayPlace because something about me told them I would understand? And what if that something they sensed was because of Emily?

Didn't that mean she lived on?

Helping others doesn't make her death worthwhile. I will never in all my life say her death was a good thing.

But good came from her life. Lots of good. More good things are coming.

Good will come from your baby's life as well. Your baby has changed you and will keep changing you. The person you are right now, and the good you do right now, is a testament to your baby's own goodness, and it's something you too will carry forward.

REACHING MORE FOR GOD

Through the whole of our journey loving Emily, I framed it in a spiritual context. I always thought of having children as a participation in the action of creation with God. We thought of children as gifts from Him, and Emily was no less a gift because of her birth defect. I've always seen crisis and suffering as a challenge by God to grow in a certain way, to a certain end, and I always kept that in mind during the pregnancy and during the grief, and later still while discerning whether and when to have more children.

I don't know what God wanted to teach me with Emily, and I don't know whether I learned it. But I did try to remain teachable during that time, so maybe.

Spiritually, my husband and I both learned more about trust. Faith when everything is working according to your plan is relatively easy; faith when it's God's plan, and you don't really understand why God's plan hurts so much—that's harder.

One day in the midst of grief, when I realized I was feeling better, I had a sudden ache. *When it hurts, I reach out for you,* I prayed, *and then you help so it doesn't hurt so much. But then I'm not reaching out for you anymore, am I? So what happens when it stops hurting? Do I just stop reaching for you?*

Fortunately I didn't do that, but for a moment while I was driving, I could see only two choices: hurt forever or abandon God because God had been so good and generous to me. It isn't that black-and-white, of course.

Maybe in the long run, what God grew in our souls during that period was fortitude. Was gratitude. Was a sense of the purpose in our suffering.

One mother said that knowing her baby is waiting for her in heaven is part of what keeps her on the right path now. She doesn't want to miss out on heaven because she already has someone there for her, waiting.

Someone else told me, early on, that I was giving birth to a saint. True: Emily will never know sin, will never know cruelty, and will never know anything but love. We loved her. God loves her. I won't say it's better this way. (I will never say it's better this way.) But maybe she's one of the Holy Innocents.

If she's our personal saint, she prays for us. Even if your denomination doesn't believe in asking saints for their prayers, remember that in the Book of Revelation we read how the saints in heaven watch the goings-on earthside. Then they pray for God to intervene in earthly affairs. Events take place on earth, and the saints and angels act in their liturgy, and then God acts on human affairs. Christians therefore can trust that their little ones are praying for them.

My husband told me one night about a favorite passage from *The Lord of the Rings*. Sam and Frodo have followed Gollum through a dangerous, swampy area. When they look back after crossing, they realize that this one horrible path they took was in fact the only way they could have gotten through the swamp. And he said to me that in a way, that's how this felt for us. That although it was hard, when we looked back, we found that this was the only way to where we were then.

Sometimes I would find myself thinking about alternate universes, and whether in another universe I'd kept Emily. Maybe in some other universe I'd managed to have both Emily and the baby who came fourteen months after Emily…and there, maybe I didn't appreciate having them both. Maybe I was just overwhelmed and tired and didn't appreciate the gift of two healthy little girls.

In the end, I don't know. It's about trust and about waiting. It's about taking our personal worst-case scenarios and working with God to turn them into best-cases. And if Rule One was loving your baby, then maybe the final outcome of following Rule One is Result One: that in eternity, you're going to meet your baby and find out how much your baby loves you too.

OTHER RESOURCES

WEBSITES

Your first online visit should be to Be Not Afraid. They provide comprehensive, practical, and peer-based support to parents experiencing a prenatal diagnosis and carrying to term. http://www.BeNotAfraid.net

Perinatal Hospice and Palliative Care provides support resources for parents and professionals.
 http://www.PerinatalHospice.Org

Perinatal Hospice and Bereavement in Northern Illinois is at http://www.thehavennetwork.org/ but have resources and links for all parents who are carrying to term.

Anencephaly.info is Monika Jacquier's site, a clearinghouse of information about anencephaly, anencephaly, and fetal acrania.

Here's Mark Shea's piece on hope for miscarried babies: http://www.ncregister.com/blog/mark-shea/hope_for_miscarried_babies

Now I Lay Me Down to Sleep is the volunteer network of professional photographers who will take photos of you and your baby. https://www.nowilaymedowntosleep.org

Plant a Memory is the current incarnation of the place where I bought my flower seed packets.
http://www.plantamemory.com/Plant-Memorial-Gifts.html

Maya Wrap is at http://www.mayawrap.com, and the kind I had was a Comfort Fit sling.

Information about the Haberman feeder if your baby may have trouble feeding from a regular bottle: http://www.mandyhaberman.com/haberman-feeder

The March of Dimes will send you a free bereavement package if you fill out the form here:
http://www.marchofdimes.org/bereavement-kit-form.aspx

Free caskets for infants are available from Trappist Caskets for those in the US. https://trappistcaskets.com/infant/

Here's an article about how some children with minimal brain tissue can still perceive sensory stimuli, respond to music, and get used to individual people:
http://hydranencephaly.com/drshewmonsarticle.htm

A medical journal found no evidence that insurance refuses to pay for patients who leave the hospital AMA:
https://www.ncbi.nlm.nih.gov/pmc/articles/PMC3378751

I am a writer with novels and short stories for sale. The stories in general have my sense of humor, so if you think you might want to spend more time hearing from me, check out http://janelebak.com/my-books. If you do want to check out my stories, please be warned that *Half Missing*, *Relic of His Heart*, "Damage," and "Winter Branches" may be too sensitive for you to read right now.

BOOKS

Waiting with Gabriel by Amy Kuebelbeck
Gabriel had hypoplastic left heart syndrome.

Letters to Gabriel by Karen Garver Santorum (not the same Gabriel)
Gabriel had anencephaly, and his story is told in letters from his mother.

When Hello Means Goodbye by Pat Schwiebert and Paul Kirk
A guide to coping with the initial throes of loss. I read this several times.

Still to Be Born by Pat Schwiebert and Paul Kirk
About the stresses and joys of a subsequent pregnancy.

The Gift of Time by Amy Kuebelbeck
Another guide to CTT by a woman who's been there.

When a Baby Dies by Rana K. Limbo and Sarah Rich Wheeler
A thorough handbook about all the issues surrounding perinatal loss.

I Will Carry You by Angie Smith
Baby Audrey had trisomy 18.

ABOUT THE AUTHOR

If you've read this whole book, you probably know more about the author than you ever wanted to know.

Jane Lebak has been publishing since 1991, with a brief break to marry and start a family. She and her husband James have four living children and one daughter waiting for them in heaven. Jane has managed an infant loss support group online and run a Carrying to Term support website in addition to publishing novels, short stories, poems, short humor, and anything else she can sell. Her work has been featured in *Liguorian Magazine, Mothering, Family Foundations*, an anthology by Ronda Chervin, and two volumes of *Chicken Soup for the Soul* (among others).

Jane talks to angels and knits socks in her spare time. If you're not sick of her by now, you can visit her website at http://www.janelebak.com.

www.ingramcontent.com/pod-product-compliance
Lightning Source LLC
Chambersburg PA
CBHW071305110526
44591CB00010B/788